MW00464381

PICKING UP THE PIECES

Live Your Best Life

A MEMOIR

MARIE JOINER

Marie Joiner

ISBN: 978-1-950621-16-3 (paperback)

ISBN: 978-1-950621-17-0 (hardback)

Published by Lighthouse Global Publishing and PR LLC

Book Formatting by Homestead Publishing Co. LLC

FOREWORD

What is my connection to Marie Joiner? What have I learned about Marie over the past 15 years? She is a remarkable, beautiful woman who has survived and thrived, as she describes in her life story, Picking Up The Pieces.

Little did I know her story when we first met when Luxury Limo Company provided a limo for my husband's birthday. Our friendship has grown over the years as she has shared pieces of her life. As she says, everyone has a story. But what strikes me as unique and so admirable is the depth of her struggles and how she has risen, much like the Phoenix from its ashes.

In learning of her sad childhood, described in Chapter 4, "12 Going on 35," I was once again impressed with her resilience and how she chose to keep pressing for more in her life. As a retired educator, I have seen many a "Marie" who succumbed to being helpless, who continued to live the cycle of poverty and dysfunction. But not Marie Joiner!

Probably what I most admire is that she realized her lack of education early on. She is a self-taught learner who realized the importance of an education and proceeded to grasp knowledge from everywhere. Her story should certainly inspire a young person who might be struggling in school to realize what doors open when you have an education.

Driven by the need to have a better life, a financially independent life, a loving life, Marie accomplished all this through setting up the limo company—now celebrating 25 years—obtaining her real estate license, and most importantly, letting herself be loved by her soulmate, Mark Joiner.

The family has had many challenges throughout the years, such as a home invasion—something few families survive—but has come through strong.

As the pieces of life's puzzle begin to come together, Marie is still driven to keep learning, expanding her world.

I strongly believe women should be supportive of each other, applaud when they succeed, and pick each other up when they fall. Together we will create stronger women who learn from each other and won't have as many pieces to pick up.

As you read this book, think of your own life and what, as women, we have to share with the next generations.

I am honored to write this foreword for my dear friend, Marie Joiner.

Pat Portwood

Not everyone will understand your journey. That's fine. It's not their journey to make sense of.

1

PICTURE PERFECT

I believe we all have a story and when we share our stories, they can bring healing to ourselves and each other. Something powerful and bigger than us can emerge from what can sometimes feel like ashes. I am not telling my own story because I want people to feel sorry for me. Nor am I writing this book because I want to publicly shame other people. My life was hard, but so are the lives of many. I desire to contribute to the idea that following trauma, we can not only persevere but thrive.

From childhood to adulthood, I have learned to be extremely resilient. I survived a horrific childhood, many brushes with death, danger, and jail, and several abusive relationships. I raised myself and my younger sister in chaotic households and weathered the storms brought on by two parents who deeply struggled. My parents did not know how to love themselves. How could I expect them to love me and my siblings?

This is a story about picking up the pieces of a broken life and learning how to be self-sustaining, self-sufficient, and strong. I used my life experiences and the experiences of others to create the life I wanted for myself, regardless of the power that anything and anyone may have had over me. You can become a product of your environment or you can break the chain so the next generation does not need to go through what you went through.

When I was asked why I wanted to write this book, the answer was immediately clear to me. I want women to know that they can start a new trajectory, whether in life, business, or finances, no matter how many factors are against them or how many roadblocks there are. There is a sense of confidence that comes from making your own money and supporting yourself. There's a sense of safety in knowing you're not dependent on a man, that no matter how unsafe your life is, you have a financial way out if you ever need it.

I hope you find strength and motivation in my story, whether it's to begin a business despite your fear, or leave a dangerous relationship that deep down you know you need to abandon. Life is tough, but you and I are both tougher than anything the world throws at us. Remember that as you read.

My name is Marie Joiner. I was born in the winter of 1964 to Richard Lee and Louise Marie Benge in Phoenix, Arizona.

My mother was 21 and already had two children when I

was born. I had an older brother, Benjamin, that she had given up for adoption when she was only 17, and my older sister Rachel, my mom and dad's first child. I did not know about my brother Benjamin until I was 15 years old. Later on, they would have one more child, Renee.

We grew up in Phoenix, in the middle of the desert. My mom and dad had built their home from the ground up, a two-story custom home built just for us against a backdrop of beautiful sunsets and desert wildlife. My sisters and I played in the dirt, chased the chickens, and had a little world of adventure on our farm in the desert. It was a great place to grow up.

This period in our lives was very peaceful and happy. My little sister Renee was still too young to remember very much. Rachel and I would later call it our "Beaver Cleaver life." We had everything we needed; we were comfortable and safe, with parents who appeared to love each other without a doubt. Later in life, when we lost what we had, we would look back on these days and wonder what of it was a lie, while also missing the innocence we experienced as small children. No matter what happened, we were protected then, both by our ages and our circumstances.

My dad was a hard worker. He had several businesses: he owned a car dealership and a vending business, and later on in life, he became a general contractor and owned his own construction company with my uncle Bill. When he was 23, and before we were born, my dad lost his leg in a motorcycle accident, and as a result of that accident, he became an alcoholic. In our earlier years, my sisters and I didn't realize Dad had a drinking problem. We had little glimpses of it. I can remember my mom putting my dad to bed after he had "too much fun." It would be a few years before we fully understood what exactly that meant.

We thought we had a perfect life up until I was about nine years old, when my mom's mom died. From that day forward, our lives were never the same. It was almost as if when my grandma died, my childhood quickly followed. This was the beginning of the end of my safety and security. Mom and Dad never raised their voices at each other in the 11 years they were married, but nonetheless, our "Beaver Cleaver life" was over. We would never be one happy family again.

Live in such a way that if your children are ever asked for the definitions of kindness, integrity, and loyalty, they'll answer, "my parents."

— Ali B. Moe

2
─────

THE GLASS WINDOW

*T*here were a lot of secrets and half-truths in my mom's life. I didn't learn until I was in my early forties that my mother grew up in a brothel run by my grandfather, grandmother, and great-grandmother. She told me when I was older how she was raped and how her mother forced her to give up her son when she was 17. I would not get to meet Benjamin until I was in my thirties. Mom had always been adamant that we were not to try and find our brother. Remember, I was 15 when I found out about him, and my sisters and I always wanted to meet him. My dad had told me about Benjamin out of spite to hurt my mother. I'm grateful because I may have never known otherwise. Mom had some fierce walls around her, but not wanting to meet one of your children never added up in my mind. Finally, as adults, we couldn't take it anymore. My sister Renee began searching for him and my mom begged her to stop. She even asked me to ask Renee to stop looking. I'm so thankful Renee persisted. When she found out how we could reach him, we were so excited. Renee and I sat together as I made the call. Our brother's wife answered and we enthusiastically shared that we were Benjamin's sisters. Our brother was so happy and shocked to find out he had sisters. He had always wondered about his biological parents, but he had never imagined he had three sisters out there. Benjamin is a wonderful person and we have a great relationship today. My mom's reasons for not wanting us to meet Benjamin became clear when we met him in person. There he stood with beautiful red hair, and he was clearly not African American. My mom's story had always been (and still is to this day) that Benjamin was conceived from her being raped by five African American men. Not a redhead. I had a cousin named Levi growing up with the same red hair as Benjamin's. Looking back, my mom always had such a strong attachment to him, and he was a redhead just like my brother.

I wonder now if her story may have been partially driven by the baby she had given up so long ago. She was pregnant young, in a time and place where teenage pregnancy was unacceptable. Maybe that's why she lied? I think she just never could face the truth that she had given up a child. It was like her to never mention the peculiarity of my redheaded brother not being black, and so acknowledge that her story didn't add up. Finding out that my mom may have been raped and then had a child she was forced to give up helped explain her behavior during that time, and all the years after. Discovering it wasn't true pointed to the possibility of other trauma. Honestly, there could be so much more or less to her story. I'm not sure if I'll ever really know. Either way, she was always so cold. It confused me. One part of me says, *She was a good mother,* but I think that comes from believing, deep down, that she loved me and my sisters. Maybe because when I balance the scales, she was less abusive than my dad? Or maybe I just feel bad saying it straight out. I think more than anything she just couldn't put what was best for us girls as children before what she wanted. But that one distinction cost my sisters and me everything we held dear. She would say that she loved me, but when she would give me a hug, I could feel the emptiness inside her. Her upbringing left a void. It feels as if she just locked herself inside a long time ago and has never been able to get back out. She locked herself in and locked me out. It was hard, feeling so disconnected from my mom. I wanted to be able to tell her things and have her listen, have her maybe hug me and tell me it was going to be okay. But that was just never going to be our story. Maybe she needed someone to do that for her too, but as it played out, we held each other at arm's length. Further, I resented every destructive choice she made for us. Each time I tried to tell her how I felt, she let me know that nothing was her fault; everything was the result of someone or something else. Her failings were because of her husband or us kids; her discontentment with life was because of her circumstances. Growing up with a mom like that motivated me to make my own way in the world, because I didn't want to live at the mercy of other people. I, unlike my mother, wanted to make my own destiny and be responsible for everything, from the house I lived in to what I had for breakfast in the morning. If I'm honest, I needed to be the opposite of her.

When my mom and dad's relationship came to an explosive head, the fallout never settled. My dad came back to the house drunk after my grandmother died. Rachel and I stood on the porch looking through the big bay window, listening to my mother scream at my dad. He'd shown up hammered driving his little El Camino. My aunt Georgia made my sister and me go outside. We could hear my mom screaming, "You've never been there for me! You're a fucking drunk!" Afterward, she locked herself in the bathroom. If I close my eyes and think back, I can still hear my uncle Ronnie saying she had fainted and hear my dad kicking in the door. To this day, I'm not sure if my mom actually did faint or if she was just acting dramatic to prove a point to my father. But I can clearly remember feeling so scared and confused about what was going on. Suddenly, a physical fight broke out in the back yard between my mom and dad. Rachel and I just kept watching through the glass window. If I had been made of glass, this is when I might have first shattered. The day my mom's mom passed marked the last day we would ever live at home as we knew it.

This was the first time in my short life that I experienced

death and divorce, but it wouldn't be the last. It was like a landslide of devastation hit. A week after my grandmother died, my grandfather died. A few months later, my 49-year-old aunt (my dad's sister) died too. To a child used to a picture-perfect life, everything completely began to unravel. I felt wide-eyed with panic. Everything I had come to know evaporated in what seemed like an instant.

Shortly after that terrible fight at my grandma's house, my mom and dad's marriage ended. In a turn of events so confusing to our little minds, my mom decided we were moving to California. Things didn't just change. We didn't just move from our old home. We watched our lives go up in flames. Not because we were moving, but because of what we were moving into. We didn't understand it then but we were entering a season of our lives that would almost take us out. Mom packed our things and we drove away from our beautiful Phoenix desert farm and made our way to the semi-small town of Modesto, California. Initially, we lived with Auntie Sharon and Uncle Bill. To me, things happened overnight, but looking back, I really think my mom had been planning on leaving my dad all along because of his alcoholism. Adult Marie understands, but as a child it was like, suddenly, I woke up from a happy dream into something that felt overwhelming and traumatizing.

My parents' separation was remarkably bitter, filled with manipulation and using us kids as the knife in the other's back. This made me very angry. It planted the seed of pain that would soon grow into rage. I vowed to pay them back for ruining our lives, and boy, did I.

Following the divorce, while we lived with our mom in California, my dad stayed back in Arizona. We enrolled in school and tried to adjust to our new normal. I couldn't shake how bad everything felt inside, no matter how much I tried not to think about it. At nine or ten years old, changing everything so quickly and, on top of that, not talking about it was a recipe for internal disaster. When summer came, my dad visited my sisters and me then took us back to Arizona with him for summer break. It felt good to be back where we grew up but nothing was the same, which left us somewhere between nerve-racked and excited. As summer neared its end, Dad wouldn't let us leave. He kept telling us we'd go back eventually, giving us a different reason every time we asked why we couldn't go back to Mom. He used this time with us to ask, almost daily, if we wanted to live with him. He'd paint a picture of how great it would be if we lived together, sometimes just asking point-blank if we'd choose to live with him instead of Mom. If you have ever been caught between two parents trying to hurt the other through their children, then you know how extremely stressful it feels. We were so young that we didn't understand the hidden agenda. I later learned all of that was technically kidnapping since my dad didn't have any legal claim to our guardianship. It was ridiculous how long it went on. We even had to re-enroll in school in Arizona. Eventually, my mom took him to court and fought for custody, accusing him of custodial interference.

As our case worked its way through the courts, it became clear to us we would have to decide whom we wanted to live with. That was pretty harrowing, being so young; we wanted the love of both parents, as any child would, and wondering what would happen to one if we chose the other really took a toll on us. Up until the court date, we had chosen my father primarily because he had been "working" on us for months. But that day, all three of us, my older sister Rachel, younger sister Renee, and I decided we'd rather stay with Mom.

There will always be people in your life who treat you wrong. Be sure to thank them for making you strong.

— *Unknown*

3

THE LESSER OF TWO EVILS

*M*om. Then Mom and Jim. As soon as my mom and Jim could legally marry after her divorce from my dad, they did. I was eager to meet Jim. I wanted to be optimistic, hoping maybe he might help make things better. I was equally afraid that I might really like him and felt it would be a betrayal of my dad. Well, bad news. Jim, like my father, was an alcoholic. Our new life with him was a far cry from our former "Beaver Cleaver" household. He and my mom both drank and partied hard. The air often felt thick with chaos and fighting. I was so angry as time went on because my mom could not explain what happened to her marriage to my dad, other than to say my father was an alcoholic and that's why she divorced him. Then she married another alcoholic, which reeked of insanity. I remember thinking, *At least my* *father wasn't violent when he was drunk.* But that would end up changing over time as well.

Anyone can have a child and call themselves a 'parent.' A real parent is someone who puts that child above their own selfish needs and wants. — Unknown

Growing up in my mother's household was violent. My stepsister, Patience, didn't like the idea that she had a new family and, looking back, I don't blame her. Jim had been married four times before he married my mom. Patience had already been through so much and suddenly she inherited *another* family. My sisters, mom and I showed up and soon after, another baby sister. Jim tried to redirect that animosity by making us go outside and fight one another. Yes, physically fight each other. How crazy! I felt so confused the first time and every time after that. I couldn't understand why he'd do that to two little girls. I would always end up on top of Patience. We would slap and pull, but I could never bring myself to punch her. I literally cannot imagine doing that to my children or anyone's children. Today, Patience and I are very close. We have a special relationship, but back then we were pitted against each other like pit bulls. I had no refuge in normality. My life kept moving further and further toward a freefall. As wild as everything was, I think I was my mom's favorite—a talented, athletic girl with the strongest of wills— and that led to me nearly always coming out on top in the end. At this point in time, the anger that had begun as an ember was rapidly fanning to a flame. My parents had flipped my life on its head and I wasn't letting it go softly into the night. My strong will would make sure they noticed that I was slowly dying inside. I may have been a child, but my feelings carried the depth and the fury of what felt like decades.

When I started smoking at the age of nine, soon after we had settled in California, I couldn't fathom that I would lose my sister Rachel over it. I had gotten my older sister Rachel and stepsister Patience to smoke cigarettes in an alley near our house. I made sure they both smoked with me so neither one would tell. Unsurprisingly, we got busted. I'm sure we weren't incredibly sneaky. Although it was my idea, Rachel ended up taking the fall for it. I could hear Jim and mom yelling at each other. I sat in the room on my bed, listening. I remember feeling like I had just gotten my sister sent away. My mom kept saying, "Rachel's got to go and I'm calling her dad to take her." I felt so sad, like it was my fault. At nine, I couldn't see how devastatingly mismatched my mom's reaction was. She was really sending Rachel away to live with our dad in Arizona. It was another loss, another decision that damaged my sisters and me. From that point on, Rachel was pretty detached from us; she felt abandoned by her family and started down a long and dangerous path of her own. I didn't learn about or witness the extent of the damage until later. The ability my mom had to let go of her children, this scary pattern of disconnect, may have begun with letting go of her firstborn. Wherever it came from, it never left. I couldn't try to psychoanalyze her back then; I just knew we all felt disconnected from mom and vice versa. It hurt so much, but I found that anger can hide the pain if you get mad enough.

Then I found an escape. A magical pill that literally numbed the pain. For a little while, I didn't have to think, feel, or remember how screwed up things had become. Some say pot is the gateway drug—for me, it was Valium. Growing up, I never hung out with anybody that was my age. My friends were 14 and 15 years old while I was barely scraping 10. The first time I got high was on Valium, supplied to me by my friends. Everything would go into slow motion—my words, my body movements. I would begin to slur as my body and my emotions went numb. After getting high, I went home, where my mom knew instantly that there was something wrong with me. I was trying to wash the dishes and I wasn't doing a very good job. By a good job, I mean I couldn't move at even a semi-normal speed. I couldn't talk right either. When she finally asked what was going on, I confessed and was forbidden from seeing those friends, Donna and Beatrice, again. Naturally, I just became sneakier and hung out with them anyway.

I had always been a tough little cookie, but something was happening inside me that I didn't know how to stop. I felt that my parents didn't care about me and I was turning a dark corner. I had lost all respect and confidence in them and I was losing it in myself at an alarming rate. My mom caught me smoking again and she decided she was going to teach me a lesson. She took off the filters of all the cigarettes in the pack she had found and told me to smoke them one after another. It was an awful experience, but it didn't make me quit. I knew then that smoking and drugs made my mother angry, and part of me resolved to keep using and smoking to hurt her, like she was hurting me. The other part of me kept doing drugs and smoking because I wanted to forget everything, even if only for a few hours at a time. I was spiraling.

We moved around so often that I attended five elementary schools in Modesto alone. I should mention that these were the days your parents weren't held liable if their child missed school or flat out didn't go. I found myself missing a lot of school. As I fell further and further behind, I became angrier and angrier. I could hardly read. Every subject was becoming so foreign I started to feel embarrassed and ashamed. I couldn't relate to kids my age. It started to feel that there was no place for me in school. I was frustrated with our unsettled life, angry with my mom for staying with a chaotic drunk, and upset at how often my mother would choose her husband over her children. I felt so alone and afraid. I didn't let them see. I began creating an iron shield around myself.

When my mother and Jim fought, they fought violently. They would scream, curse, and break table legs over each other. My younger sister Renee, stepsister Patience, and I would see Jim and mom completely out of control in our living room, surrounded by our green '70s furniture, fighting on too many occasions to count. Fortunately, my half-sister Charity was still so little she doesn't remember. At one point they played tug-of-war with Charity. Patience was Jim's daughter but Charity belonged to both of them. Their fighting terrified me. Prior to my grandmother's death, when my parent's marriage and my whole life started falling apart, I had no idea my mother could even raise her voice. I had never seen or heard her and my father fight, and yet here she was, brawling with the man she had chosen to marry. At the beginning of their relationship, I felt Jim was worse than my dad because he was also violent. My father would get drunk and sloppy, sure, but when I was really young, his alcoholism never turned to blows. Eventually, however, Dad became violent and at some point, I just stopped comparing.

From every wound, there is a scar, and every scar tells a story. A story that says, 'I have survived.' Turn your wounds into wisdom.

– Craig Scott

4

12 GOING ON 35

*A*t the age of 12, I got a second chance to choose whom I wanted to live with. This was the kind of power that I wanted in my hands—the chance to make my own choices, as ill-advised as that was for a lost kid. I also wanted to do the most damage to my mother, whom I still blamed for shattering our life. As I mentioned, my father also had a lot to do with influencing my decision. He had moved to Modesto when I was about 11, and he was relentless in telling me that he wanted me to live with him. That made me feel wanted and loved, but I later learned this was just to hurt my mother. I chose to leave, despite my mother on her hands and knees begging and pleading with me to stay. It may have been the sincerest display of emotion that I had ever experienced from my mom. It was too late. I had two years under my belt of violence, screaming, fighting, drinking, and moving from place to place. I moved in with my father. This decision defined my life for decades to come. But at the time, I didn't think about any of that. I was pissed off at my mother and I was going to pay her back for the hurt she was causing me. And I wanted to get out of the disaster I was living in. I don't know how many times she would tell me that she wished my dad would die, that she wished he would drive his truck off a cliff and kill himself. The way she would talk about my dad created so much stress inside of me. I knew she meant it every time she expressed how deeply she loathed him and wished him dead. Yeah, I couldn't take it anymore. So what more fitting payback than going to live with him and Rachel whom she had already kicked out, a decision I knew would make my mother heartsick. And I would be free.

Despite my high hopes of escape, my father's house was in no way any better than my mother's home. In fact, it was a lot worse. My older sister Rachel and I were free indeed. Free to do whatever we wanted there: smoke our cigarettes, get high, skip school. This only contributed to a chaotic environment that left us feeling unsettled and unmoored. At the same time, as adolescents, not having any boundaries gave us our own sense of control. And when things feel that far out of control, even the illusion of it feels better.

The first year I lived with my father would be another turning point in my life. Twelve years old was a big year for me. In the course of one year, I would run away, overdose, go to jail, and be sexually assaulted.

The overdosing came first. There was a guy named Steve who told my friends, my sisters, and me about a plant we could smoke and get high from, just like pot. It grew in a field and all we had to do was go pick some. Steve worked at the 76 gas station on the corner of Oakdale and Surry Road. In that same parking lot, you could find Jack's Liquors and Lord Byron's pizza parlor in Modesto. My stepdad Jim worked at Jack's Liquors. It faced Oakdale Road and Lord Byron's Pizza sat just behind it. This was one of my dad's watering holes that we would frequent after he would get off work, because he could take us girls there. In the middle of all three of these places was an open field that grew a beautiful plant with a big white flower. And under the leaf, there were little balls that had tiny porcupine needles. This was the part of the plant you could boil or dry out the seeds and smoke them. It was an extremely potent, dangerous hallucinogenic drug, jimsonweed, a form of belladonna that could have killed all of us. Of course, I had no idea. Steve not only told us where to find it, he told us how to boil it and consume it for a full psychoactive effect. We went out to the field where we had learned the flower grew and picked a bagful. My dad was in the pizza parlor and as soon as he was ready to go, we went home. Being the crazy kids we were at that age, we went straight home to boil and drink it. At one point as we were in the kitchen, my dad asked us girls what we were doing. We told him we were getting something to eat. We finished cutting it and started boiling the plant up. It smelled and tasted just like squash. Once we were finished, we went to Rachel's room. We all sat on the bed with our tall, green plastic glasses filled to the rim. Soon after, the effects began to settle in. Everything became distorted and slow, and soon we would be hallucinating. A nearby neighbor had gotten into some trouble with the police and coincidentally the police were right outside my dad's house in the alley. The police found me outside in the alley talking to the back of one of their police cars. They brought me back to the house and found my dad passed out, and Lela talking to the back of the toilet seat. This must have been a bizarre scene: five girls high on hallucinogens, talking to inanimate objects, with the only adult at home passed out drunk in the living room. I must have been a sight—a 12-year-old girl having what she believed was a real conversation with the back of a police car. A police car, of all things! Once they got my dad up, they rushed us all to the hospital. The doctors could not do anything for us because no one would tell them what we were on. My mom and dad loaded me in the back seat of the car and took me to a local women and children's shelter, Hutton House, in downtown Modesto next to St. Stanislaus Church. I sat in a little room on the bed, watching the wall melt in my mind's hazy eye. I needed to escape to let my parents know what I was on. The hallucinogens were so powerful I was positive that I had to unlock at least five locks on the door to get out. In reality, I just turned the doorknob and ran. I found myself running and then walking down the street toward home, which was miles away. When the Indians smoked their peyote and they said they saw the gods, this must have been how they felt. I still remember some of those hallucinations vividly, and I also remember all the people I must've scared on my way home that night. Trying to make it back to my dad's home, I started hitchhiking. A man and lady picked me up. They would only take me to the corner of Scenic and Oakdale Road, which was close to where I was trying to go but not quite there. When they dropped me off, I saw Auntie Sharon and Uncle Bill in their green El Camino. They told me my parents were not home and that they were not out looking for me either. They were at the pizzeria. When I walked in, I found them standing at the bar talking, possibly about me, but nonetheless my dad was having a drink. When I told them what we had taken, they called my friends' parents and took Rachel, Renee, and me back to the hospital. Renee was only nine years old and her blood pressure was high from the little bit she had drunk. Rachel was fine because she didn't drink enough, but they had to pump my stomach. At this point, in my opinion, my mother should have YANKED US OUT OF OUR DAD'S HOME. But she didn't. She took Renee home and Rachel and I went home to my dad's.

I ran away for the first time that same year with my older sister Rachel, our friend Bobby, and Rachel's boyfriend, Brian. I don't even remember what we had gotten in trouble for, but we decided to hit the open road. We were headed to Nevada. We were four dumbass kids. We hitchhiked out to a place called Modesto Reservoir. They had drained it that year.

I can remember the dirt being dry and cracked where the water normally rested. It looked desolate. We headed for the foothills, walking for hours until we got to a little hill with a big rock formation sticking out of the ground. We got so tired and hungry. Night one was rough. At this point, it was getting dark and we'd decided that we were not going to make it to Nevada. Since it was getting dark, we had to sleep there, out in the middle of nowhere. We had nothing to keep us warm, no food or water. We were all scared, afraid of getting bitten by rattlesnakes, coyotes, and other wild animals that might be out there. You could hear the coyotes in the distance, howling. It was getting cold as well. So we all huddled together in a spoon-like position on the hard, rocky ground. Between the mixture of fear and freezing, we didn't sleep very much that night. As soon as the sun started to rise, we began our journey back home. We came upon a ranch in the middle of the foothills. There was a little house with horses and a truck that had still had the key in the ignition. After deciding against taking the horses or the truck, we ended up breaking into the house. The door was open with only the screen closed. Rachel and I went inside while the guys kept watch. After rummaging through the refrigerator, we made off with only eggs, a small frying pan, and some matches. We rushed out of the house and we all ran as fast as we could to get as far away from the house as possible. We climbed up a hill to remain hidden and to build a fire, but it was so windy that the fire kept being blown out. We were starving. We finally got the fire started, cracked the eggs, and put them in the pan, but since it was so windy, sand blew into the eggs and rendered them inedible. Needless to say, we were still hungry. We're lucky we didn't catch the whole place on fire. There was dry grass as far as the eye could see. We began walking back and after what seemed like forever, it was getting dark again. We'd managed to make our way back to the Modesto Reservoir. We'd spotted a home, stopped, and knocked on the door but no one would answer. Eventually, a lady came to her kitchen window. We told her we were hungry and she asked us what we were doing out there. We made up an elaborate lie, I'm sure. She said she'd be right back. Time passed and I sensed she was calling the police. When she came to the window, she gave us all apples. We felt like Hansel and Gretel. Something was wrong. As soon as she gave us the apples, we took off running into a walnut orchard. Sure enough, she called the police, and we could see them coming up the road. After traipsing through orchard after orchard until the sun came up the next day, it was time to go home. We started to hitchhike. I was so tired and hungry I was crying. I just wanted to go home. We had the guys hide in the orchard while my sister and I flagged a ride down. Finally, a little white truck pulled over and a man told us girls to get in and told the boys to get in the back of the truck. He gave us a ride all the way home. We had been gone for three days and two nights. My dad barely noticed. This is the kind of parental guidance we had.

The next time I ran away, I was gone for a month. My

friend Diana and I started trying to hitchhike out of Modesto to San Andreas after we were busted for stealing her parent's car and taking it for a joyride. We were attempting to avoid getting into more trouble, and leaving town for a while seemed like a good option. When a police officer stopped us early on in our getaway, we thought for sure we were done and would be made to return home. He put us in the back of the police car and called in to see if we had been reported as runaways. We thought for sure he was going to take us in. Much to our surprise, after telling the officer a long story about us trying to get to our parents in San Andreas (which was, of course, entirely made up), he let us go on our way. So we started hitchhiking and made it to Farmington, California, to the old general store and saloon. There we found an old man who gave us our next ride. He had an old car. It looked like it was on its last leg. I had a bad feeling because we were headed out of town in the middle of nowhere, but he dropped us off about 15 miles before San Andreas. We finally made it to Diana's friend's house. The first night we stayed in her barn, sleeping in two recliners. The friend brought us out a couple of jackets; still, we were freezing all night. She told us that we could stay for the night but we must go the next day, not wanting to get in trouble with her parents for harboring runaways. The next few days we stayed down by the river, sleeping outside. We had no money, no clothes, and no food, but we made our way for just over a month. Diana had more friends in Valley Springs, Mickey and Dudley, and we stayed with them for the next three weeks. Diana was ready to go back about a week before I was. She traveled home first without me. I lasted about another week before turning myself in at the San Andreas jail. My mom had reported me missing by then, but because I was so far away from home, they booked me for the night. The jail reminded me of the ones I had seen in old western movies. It was enclosed with bars on three sides and one brick wall. I sat on the single cot looking through the cell bars. It was cold and I was afraid. I was brave at 12 years old, but jail really scared me. I didn't really get in trouble with my parents for that; I think they were just so grateful I was alive.

I also spent time in jail both for running away a third time and for wandering around high on crystal PCP (another dangerous drug) with my friend Donna. The third time I went to jail was because I ran away again. I think at this point my parents were trying to get me under control so they put me in juvenile hall. This really shook me. After the juvenile officers booked me, took my fingerprints and my pictures, I was then placed in my own cell. I would have been scared at any age but at 12 years old, I was terrified. The room had four walls with a cement bed, a thin mattress, and a toilet in the corner of the room. The room had five blocked windows in it. I could stand on the bed and look outside. When they shut the solid metal door with a tiny little window behind me, my heart sank and I remember crying. I could hear the other doors opening and closing. I cried all night. I stayed the night and my dad came and got me the next day.

However, I had not learned my lesson yet and went to jail again.

I would get into trouble several times after this. I eventually ended up on probation at 14 years old and remained on probation until I turned 18. At this point, I was just trying to survive being 12.

One's dignity may be assaulted and vandalized but it can never be taken away unless it's surrendered.
    — Michael J. Fox

5

MONSTERS IN THE CLOSET

*I*t took me a long time to fully acknowledge what happened to me while living with my dad. I don't know that I fully understood how young I really was surviving what I survived until I saw my own daughter playing when she was 12 and 13 years old. She was a little girl, and maybe for the first time, I saw that I had been just a little girl at that age too. I think sometimes we can be so used to our own story that it's often through the eyes of someone else we might realize that our story is in fact shocking.

My dad was a mess, and because I lived with him, I had no boundaries, rules, or restrictions, which is how I was able to go so far into chaos and heartbreak. He wasn't just a mess—he was a black hole. Just being near him invited what would become my darkest memories. I had hardly had a first kiss when he began calling me a whore. My sisters and I were called many names, and rarely by our real ones. Sometimes he would even call us his boys. When he moved to Modesto, he'd become a contractor and started a cement company with my uncle Bill. I will give him this—he was a hard worker and he always owned his own companies. As a businesswoman today who successfully owns my own companies, I can't give him credit for my business acumen, but I will say that's the one thing I respect about him. He had a crew of cement masons in their 20s, 30s, and 40s who stayed at our house with a revolving door. These men were rough and some were just getting out of prison. Many were bikers, on drugs, and drinking around the clock. How they worked and got jobs done I will never know. But they did, and there was a party every day and night at Dad's. Not the fun kind with music and cake but the kind with heroin and the sound of bottles banging. My sister Rachel and I became very skilled at helping them shoot up. We knew exactly how long to hold the lighter under the spoon so the heroin would melt down and easily be drawn up by the needle. After we'd fill the syringe with heroin, we'd tap on the side to get all the air out. We would tie the tourniquet on their arm just right, so that we could find the best vein while tapping on the vein with our finger to bring it to the surface. Then we'd take the needle, put it in their vein, and shoot the heroin in until the needle was empty.

The fridge was never stocked with food for lunches or for any meals. But if we wanted drugs or alcohol, it was stocked full. Our home was one of the biggest drug houses in Modesto. Gary and Larry, two crew members who lived with us full time, sold their drugs from our home. I didn't go to school. I was hungry most of the time and I'm not sure how I had clothes and shoes. But I had a roof over my head. Helping the guys with their drugs made me feel grown up, and it was an important job (they would say) so I didn't mind doing it.

I never did heroin myself. I saw what would happen to them when they'd nod off or get violently ill as they'd come down. I did everything else but never heroin; I knew you could get hooked by trying it even just once.

I was asleep in my bed the first time one of the guys crept into my room. I was paralyzed with fear. My heart was pounding out of my chest. The knot in my throat choked out any sound I wanted to make. I wanted to scream for help! Someone help me! His hands touched my body everywhere as I played dead and squeezed my eyes tightly shut. No one would help me. I knew I was alone. I had known for several years now that no one was coming to save me. I also knew that if I screamed, he would make it worse. I could see through my squinted eyes that Jimbo was drunk and panting on top of my 12-year-old body. He smelled like alcohol and stale cigarettes. I hate that smell to this day. I was in so much pain, my body was shaking with fear, but I held the tears back. *If I stay quiet and don't fight, he won't hurt me more.* Fear doesn't describe what coursed through my veins. So many pieces of me fell to the floor that night. He was the first but he wasn't the last. No matter how many times I showered I still felt dirty and disgusting. No matter how many pieces of furniture I pushed in front of my bedroom door, they still came in. I was plagued with feeling that somehow it was my fault. Today, I know that couldn't be further from the truth. Rape is never the victim's fault. I was a child. Jimbo was the first to rape me but when I realized I couldn't make them all stop I did what I had to do. I committed to a relationship with Jimbo. He was twice my age but I had done the math. It was either just him or maybe someone worse. I knew he would protect me. Sex became a job for me — a way to feel like I had a shred of control over what was happening. I began drinking and partying more than I would have ever dared. Sometimes I can see that I wasn't afraid to die back then. A part of me even welcomed the idea as a means for the pain to stop.

My dad became violent and would try to beat my sister Rachel and me. He was never in his right mind. I will never know how many nights my sister and I sat in the parking lot just outside of the bar waiting to drive Dad home at two o'clock in the morning. Being only 12 and 13 years old, we made the most of it, talking to people through the truck windows before they would go into the bar. There were so many nights after we would get home from the bar when we'd have to leave Dad in the truck because he had passed out. When he would wake up, he'd be violent and try to come into the house to beat us girls. I can't say that my sister and I didn't torment him back. We were children and tried to fight back in our own way. We would lock him out of the house and throw eggs at him if we could find them. There would be other times when he'd tell us to go to the store and get cigarettes for him, giving us notes to buy them, and letting us take his truck. Sometimes we'd stay at the store longer than we should and he would call the cops on us. The officers would pick us up and bring us back to the house, but when we'd get home he'd be passed out and they would just drop us off.

Occasionally, we'd come through the front door after being gone, just to find him passed out half-naked on the floor. Other times we'd wake up in the middle of the night and find him standing in our room, peeing in our dresser drawers, thinking he was in the bathroom. There were times when he tried to beat us, but we'd take his artificial leg from him and hide it. We had started to become him.

We had started to lose all respect for him. On several occasions, we would roll him off the couch when he was passed out drunk. If he didn't wake up from the fall, we would take his keys out of his pocket and take his truck. We would go on a joyride or we would visit Rachel's boyfriend across town.

Things had become completely out of control. The iron wall around me and my heart grew thicker by the day. I pushed the pain of my reality deep down as far as I could. If it would boil up, I would take another drink or find another line. I had to make it through somehow.

My dad knew what was happening to me and he wasn't

going to help me. It's tempting to blame it on the drugs and the alcohol—the fact that he was never in his right mind—but it was more than that. He went out of his way to hurt me. It was like he had something to prove. His friends and employees used him, used his home like a halfway house, used his children, and still, they came first no matter what. It felt like he wanted to prove he was a "man." Everything else came first and my sisters and I came last. One time, I had gone to the store with his friend Gary when police lights went on behind our car. Gary refused to pull over and kept driving back to our house. It was clear there was a problem. It turned out Gary had a warrant out for his arrest. He got to the front of our house, slowed down enough to jump out, ran into our house, and vanished. I was sitting next to him and had to put the car in park. When I was questioned by the police about the whereabouts of Gary, I wanted to be honest. I didn't know where he was but I wanted to answer their questions. After they left, my dad laid into me. He was enraged that I would talk to the police about his friends. My dad sent me to my room. I was crying, confused as to why I had gotten into trouble. As I was lying there crying, I heard a whisper coming from my closet. "Are they gone yet?" It was Gary hiding in my closet. There was some humor to it if we can look past the encapsulating dysfunction. But this was the norm—horrible chaos ensuing with my dad and his friends, and me being screamed at or worse if I tried to do anything normal. One night we were coming home from the pizza parlor, and in the distance, we could see smoke coming from our neighborhood. We all looked at each other and said, "I think it's our house!" Sure enough, it was. Gary, strung out on heroin, had fallen asleep with a cigarette and caught my bedroom on fire. Gary and Larry were twins. Rachel and I would call them our brothers. We didn't know we had a real brother yet. My dad wasn't even mad at Gary for lighting our house on fire. Dad's version of a "man" created a nasty blueprint for the type of men I allowed in my life. He set the bar so low that I didn't know the difference between love and abuse. I became a determined survivor. My dad's hatred for my mom may have been projected toward me. Some part of me knew even then that the terrible way he treated me was a profoundly misdirected attempt to hurt my mom. My anger toward both my mom and dad covered wounds that I couldn't address until years later. Back then it just felt like "kill or be killed" for me. As I mentioned, I had started a serious relationship with Jimbo. By the time I turned 13, things had become very violent and abusive with him. The irony was I had chosen to be with him because I knew he would stop all of the other men from trying to assault me if I was his girlfriend, but I still had to cope with the assaults from him. I didn't feel 13 years old and Jimbo didn't seem nearly twice my age. But when I think of it plainly, he was a pedophile and my first serious relationship was with the first man who had raped me. And I stayed with him so he would protect me from the others. He told me he loved me. I even found myself living with him at one point to escape my dad's house, but his drug use and alcoholism continued to escalate and so did mine. Once, in front of all our friends, high on acid, he tried to choke me to death, his drug-addled mind convincing him I had done something wrong. That was it for me. I didn't want to end up like my mother, stuck in a relationship with someone who thought it was okay to hurt me. But despite my determination to not become my mother's daughter, I repeatedly found myself in relationships where I would be abused and hurt and abandoned, not because I did anything to deserve it, but because I was so desperate for the love I didn't receive from my parents that I was willing to tolerate a lot—more than I should have—to get it.

I remember asking myself so often why my life spiraled out of control like this, from our neat little home in Phoenix to a chaotic upbringing where I was allowed to wander free, endure abuse, and make trouble in an already out-of-control environment. I didn't have anyone to fall back on—not even my older sister, Rachel, who was stuck in the same cycles as I was. She'd often leave me alone in dangerous places to go hook up with guys or get high. I lived life with a mix of fear and anger running through me at all times. Then, one sentence spoken by a stranger changed the trajectory of my life.

I was out with a friend of mine one day, talking about my parents and how they were treating me. I was sincerely asking God how I ended up where I was. *Why are these people my parents? Please, God, get me out of here.* An old man overheard me and interjected, "It doesn't matter who your parents are, because after you turn 18, your life is your own and you're responsible for your own choices and consequences." It was a strangely profound thing to come from this short, older man with wild, blonde bushy hair, but maybe that's why I remember it so well. Hearing that from a total stranger gave me hope. Hope that my parents wouldn't always have control over me, hope that I would someday have power and agency that I didn't have at the moment. Even now, I tell this to my nephews: you're responsible for your own choices, and a bad choice today doesn't mean you can't encounter a turning point tomorrow. It's up to you. I clung to those words and made a silent vow, *When I turn 18, I am going to change my life.* And I meant it with every fiber of my being. This life I was living was not going to be the rest of my life.

Now, looking back as an adult and as a mother of children myself, I realize that the anger I felt and the rebelliousness I displayed were both just instances of fear coming out sideways. Children need structure to thrive, and the insecurity I experienced without that structure gave me an internal sense of imbalance and chaos that I couldn't articulate but that constantly frustrated me. I wanted to be loved and wanted, and I had neither of those things. I wanted to be safe. I did a lot of things in the name of survival. I tolerated extreme abuse from boyfriends growing up because I felt I needed safety and shelter. Eventually, homelessness became safer than living at home.

I believe in God not because my parents told me, not because my church told me, but because I've experienced His goodness and mercy myself.

Amen.

6

I BUILT A DOOR

J was homeless for much of my adolescence. As things progressively worsened at my dad's, my mom's home remained violent and unstable, and food became less and less accessible, I began house-hopping. I was 13 when I began going from home to home, sleeping on friends' couches and eating their parents' food. I often found a roof to go over my head, sometimes a car. Sometimes I had to sleep on the streets. Homelessness isn't just about the streets, though— homelessness is having no place to call home. I didn't have a little safe room waiting for me anywhere. No young tween posters of silly crushes on a wall. No radio to play my favorite mix cassette tapes. No bedtime or dinnertime. No one staying up late, worrying about where I was or if I was okay. I had myself and whatever I could come up with to take care of myself. I was a child trying as hard as I could to keep it together. But bad things happen to kids on the streets. I would end up in cars with people who were essentially strangers, in places that were so dangerous. I recall riding with a few people I didn't really know one night. We arrived at a party in the middle of nowhere. A man in his 30s assaulted me and I couldn't stop him because I was too small and too afraid. My life had become about desperately trying to take care of myself. In case you are wondering about school, I had stopped going entirely. I barely made it through fifth grade and that was it. I was out in the world on my own and it had become purely about survival. I continued to cultivate a very strong exterior, but inside it just kept getting harder to get up and fight every day.

Around 14, I started to realize how much I hated living the way I was. I mean, I had hated it from the second things began to unravel at nine years old, but at this point, I desperately wanted out. I wanted to escape to stability. My sister and I had lost our innocence when our life went up in flames, but we were still kids. I was also on probation and had to answer to a probation officer. This helped me to begin steering slowly into a better direction. I gained a positive influence in my life as well, in Karen, and I began staying with her. Karen was my friend Tammie's older sister's friend. I had met her a few years earlier and will never forget seeing all of her high heel shoes. This is where my obsession with high heel shoes came from. If anyone knows me, they know I love my heels. This is where I got my sense of style. Karen had a positive attitude and was good for me. She'd given me a lot of advice throughout my childhood. One of the things I could always remember her saying to me was, "Just take baby steps." She'd also tried to help me get emancipated to get away from my father. I had nowhere to go to be around positivity or kids my age. Karen introduced me to Charlie Tuna's. Charlie Tuna's created a little piece of life for me that felt safe and happy. It was a great place for kids. It was the disco era. I joined the dance team there and I was allowed to be a kid. I found some self-esteem in that environment and was able to think more highly of my potential. I was given the opportunity to do some modeling around this time as well. I would get to go to San Francisco for the print shoots, and I started to dream a little. The city made me think bigger for myself. I just loved it there. I felt like I could be somebody. This was critical timing because, in all honesty, I was incredibly suicidal at this time in my life. I remember praying so often to God—begging Him to help me get out of the life I was living. To this day, I thank God every day for saving me. I didn't feel like I belonged anywhere. But there were little things that gave me such big hope.

Both Rachel and I had fully realized how abusive our dad was and we had lost all respect for him. We wanted nothing to do with him or his disgusting friends. I had been virtually homeless for nearly two years, and I'd been to hell and back. I was exhausted. I tried to move back in with my mom when I was 15, motivated mostly by a desire to get away from some of the chaos, but I knew it was bad there too. I didn't feel welcome at my mom's and you could cut the tension with a knife. But I had just survived so much worse. So I just looked the other way when things got ugly, until I realized I had just traded in one father figure's horrible friends for another's. Not too long after I had begun staying with my mom again, we went on a fishing trip to Fox Grove. A fishing trip felt like a nice, normal family thing to do. Except that one of my stepfather's 60-year-old friends, Joe, tried coming onto me during the fishing trip. Joe asked me to help him get firewood, and I thought nothing of it and went. As we walked, he put his arm around me and tried to kiss me. I was barely 15. He had a reputation for being creepy but he blew past creepy when he touched me. When we got back to the campfire site, I sat quietly for the rest of the trip, withdrawn. I felt stressed and on guard the entire time, and I kept my distance. A couple of days after we got home, my mom told me we were going to move next door to Joe. I decided to tell my mom and Jim about what had happened. Jim didn't believe me. My mom did, but I knew she wouldn't put her foot down on my behalf. When Jim refused to budge and said we were moving next door to Joe anyway, I ran away again rather than stay there. Was there not anywhere I could go and be safe? I'd rather stay homeless and deal with the threats that came from the streets than live in another home with parent figures who didn't care about me. Out on the streets, it made sense to feel alone, scared, or unloved, but feeling that way with my "family" triggered rage and despair. No. I could not live with either of them.

The night I ran away, Gary and Larry lived about five blocks away. I walked to their house but they weren't home. Two guys pulled up in the court in a blue Nova. I didn't know them, but they offered me a ride to a party in Sonora. It's clear I did things like that a lot back then, but this time, I had an awful feeling in my gut, like something bad was about to happen. As we drove down Warnerville Road, one of the guys kept putting his arm around me and trying to kiss me. All of us, including the driver, were drinking.

The driver lost control of the car as we were going around a 15-mph corner and broke his arm when the car crashed into a ditch. It sounds silly, but I was thankful for the car accident. *God saved me again.* I don't think I would've come back from that party. I think those guys had plans for me that didn't involve me ever returning to Modesto. We had to drive back to Modesto to Doctors Hospital and drop the driver off. The other guy dropped me off and I snuck back into my mom's house after that accident. I think my mom knew I had been gone, but all she asked was why I was wearing my clothes from the night before. I told her I was cold and left it at that. We were both so far past honest communication. Our exchanges had become a pure formality and we both knew it. A couple of days later, I ran away again. This time, it would be several years before I came back.

I spent some of this time homeless again and couch-hopping, which was arguably easier and more predictable than living in either parent's house. My life was so dangerous during my adolescence. Even though I didn't realize it then, the behaviors in which I was engaging were risky and life-threatening. When I went to court to see if I could get emancipated, I was told I couldn't because I didn't have a reliable way to support myself.

I eventually began dating my most violent boyfriend yet. Chris was 21 and I was 15 going on who knows how old at this point. It wasn't a big decision for me to move in with him as I was already without a steady place to stay. My radar was finely tuned to violent addicts who were older than me and Chris was exactly that. He called me names and treated me like he owned me. I loved/hated him, and mostly I felt trapped. This went on until I was almost 18. At 16, I became pregnant. I eventually chose to have an abortion because I couldn't imagine how I would care for a baby as a teenager with no real home and being in the relationship I was in. Chris supported the decision. When I went to my mom to ask for her advice, she told me I needed to make my own decisions, without any offer of support. When I left the clinic, I felt like I had experienced a loss that could never be fully expressed. I lost a piece of me that is irreplaceable and what little respect I had for myself. I really needed someone safe to process what I had been through but there was no one to talk to. Things with Chris and me continued to escalate to points where I wasn't sure if I would make it out alive—physically or emotionally. A little time passed and I became pregnant again. This time I would not have an abortion. I made what felt like the ultimate sacrifice. Chris was losing his place and because I was pregnant, we needed a place to stay. We moved in with my dad. I had managed to stay away from my dad as much as possible over the previous few years, but he had gotten even worse. Chris and I had terrible fights but one night, in particular, was by far the most damaging. Chris came home angry, drunk, and jealous, and he proceeded to beat the shit out of me and everything I owned. He even broke out all the windows in our apartment, then he took a billy club and broke out every window in my 1972 blue Riviera. And then my dad, in a moment I'll never forgive him for, pushed a chair in front of the door so I couldn't get away, and he told Chris to beat me more. Chris did, and my dad watched and even continued to egg him on. Our next-door neighbors called the police. Chris went to jail for about five days, and I became homeless again. I lost the baby and Chris and I were officially over soon after. I was tired of the abuse, so I left him and moved into an old warehouse, promising myself I would never go back to Chris.

I took my little sister Renee with me and we moved into the warehouse that my friend Bruce rented. It wasn't much, but it was the safest we'd been for some time. It had no electricity and no bathroom, but it had a potbelly stove we could cook on and we could boil water so we could take a bath with a big pot we'd found. If we needed to use the restroom, we had to go outside in the nearby field. We lived there for about six months. I remember being immensely thankful when I could take Renee out of my father's house and give her an environment that was at least a little more peaceful. She didn't really witness much of the chaotic life my dad, our sister Rachel, and I had led; she'd only lived with him for a year and a half. And I had spent most of that time protecting her from the violence and abuse that went on.

A few months later, my dad figured out where we lived and he showed up, drunk off his ass. He had been living at his girlfriend's house down the street and had gotten into a fight with her. So he came to the warehouse and passed out in the back of his car. Renee discovered this and began running around his car saying, "My dad is an alcoholic. My dad is an alcoholic." She was taunting him and he woke up furious. He got out of his car, took his belt off and was about to start hitting her with it. I stood in front of her and he hit me in my face with the belt buckle, then my leg and my back as he wildly swung. That was the first time I actually hit back. As the saying goes, I saw red; I took all of my aggression and rage and unleashed it on him, knocking him to the ground and going berserk until my sister had to pull me off him. *There was no way in hell*, I remember thinking, *that he was going to hurt my baby sister*. Before it was all over, I had a black eye, welts, and bruises all over my body.

This was my turning point. I was 17 and going to turn 18 in a month. I was getting off probation and I knew I needed to change my life. I remember looking down at him, drunk and on the ground, and thinking, *How pitiful*. He got up and walked away with his head down, back toward his girlfriend's house. I did not see my dad for several years after that.

I realized then that if I didn't change things right then, I was going to be just like him for the rest of my life. That scared me more than most things I had endured up until that point. I heard that old man's voice in my head saying, *You are responsible for your own life after you turn 18*, and that reassured me. I was in charge of my own world, and I proved it for the first time when I was finally able to protect my sister. I called my mom and asked if I could come and talk to her. I told my little sister I was going home and she needed to come with me. She didn't want to at first. I said, "Well, I'm going. If you don't want to go, you'll have to go to juvenile hall. But I am going home."

My mom agreed to see me. She was shocked to see me in the condition I was in. I weighed 80 pounds and looked anorexic, bruises from head to toe, and a black eye. The first thing she did was call the police and make a report. The police came and took the report and took pictures of all of my injuries.

My mom and stepdad Jim told Renee and I that we couldn't live there. We could stay the night but had to leave the next day. I didn't really blame them. I'd done so much to break my mom's heart. The next day, before we were to leave, they came to us and said we could stay under one condition.

We would need to sign a contract with rules and regulations that we had to go by. At this point, rules sounded good. I knew this was not going to be easy because I'd been on my own for so long, but I was going to try. Being homeless had made me feel worthless, sad, and filthy. I was so messed up. I was a broken human being, mentally and physically. I had hope for the first time in a very long time. Believe me, it wasn't easy to live by all the rules, but Karen's advice played in my head: "Just baby steps."

I still drive through the areas I grew up in and sometimes I'll sit and reflect in front of the house where I lived. Although I am so grateful for the life I have now, occasionally old memories haunt me. Sometimes it's the simple things that hurt, like the fact that I could never buy a card or gift for my parents, the way my husband would for his. What would I say? "Thanks for the good life you gave me"? I provided a good, stable life for myself years later, after I learned some terribly hard lessons. Still, I firmly believe I was able to endure all of that because my childhood gave me strength.

From the time I started trying to positively alter the course of my life, up until now, there have been moments and interactions that have reminded me of the person I used to be and the life I used to live. Most of those memories come from the family members I still speak to. It feels like that life was a totally different life — one that doesn't even intertwine with the one I live now.

It's sadly ironic, looking back, that my little sister Renee was the least screwed up among the three of us girls, but now she's the one who is struggling the most. It was devastating to watch her steadily spiral downward. There comes a point in everyone's life where no one can save you but yourself, and Renee has long since passed that point. Still, I felt—and still feel—differently about her struggles than I did about my parents. Renee is my baby sister; I still feel like it's my job to protect her and it's hard to reckon with the knowledge that I can't.

I wasn't able to pass my strength on to Renee, but I did get that chance with her daughter, Tabatha. She lived a life like mine and I saw that in her, so I took her in. I gave her one chance to get her life together. I gave her a place to live, a car to drive, and six months to get it together. I told her, "As long as you're moving forward, I'm moving forward with you." I wanted to give her a place to go when she backslid, and support to get back on her feet—something I never had. It was important to me that I gave her a place where she could lay her head and feel welcome. I didn't have that when I couch-surfed, secure in nothing but the knowledge that I was an unwelcome guest. I wanted better for my niece, who was clearly trying so hard to get her life back on track. I have actually helped quite a few young kids and adults to get their lives moving forward. It's been my way of trying to help others in the ways that might have helped me.

Go back to 18-year-old Marie. Staying true to my vow of changing my life at 18, I was willing to do whatever it took. I signed the contract and lived by their rules. I was willing to do that because I kept remembering that moment when I stood over my father and realized that if I didn't change my life now, it would most likely never change.

I still partied and used drugs after moving back in with Mom, but I was on a new path. I remember a few nights when my mom had to help me to bed when I was high, but she never said anything to Jim so I could keep living there. Even though I was the most troubled, I know she felt the most connected to me, and as I've shared, she's not the "connected" type. I still kept her at a distance. I was angry. Angry that my life was screwed up, angry that my parents didn't seem to love us enough to take care of us. I was specifically angry with my mom for not fighting harder for me with my father. Back then and even now Mom and I were never going to see eye to eye. Now, I have empathy and compassion that have melted the walls around my heart, but it took years. For a long time, you couldn't get any emotion out of me other than anger, usually accompanied by physical violence. When I lived with my mother, she and I were locked in a pattern of distance. My mother has never been an empathetic person. She always told me I needed to make life-altering decisions for myself whether or not I wanted to. Meaning, she didn't stop me from going on the path I chose because I needed to find out for myself. Looking back, as a mother myself, I understand her desire to raise a self-sufficient child, but every daughter needs her mother, and I never had mine. She can say it was a lesson, but in the end, her children were harmed almost beyond repair. That's not a lesson—that's abandonment. So I maintained my "tough guy" reputation for not crying. I was strong, and I chose to be that way because I was tired of being taken advantage of. I would never live at the mercy of another man or person again. My body and self-image really took a nosedive by the time I began turning my life around. At 80 pounds, I used to joke that not even size zero clothes fit me. And while most people thought I was pretty, I always felt like I was ugly. I think part of that stemmed from the fact that my body had been so violated. Sex wasn't something I did for love; it was just a thing I did for safety or to protect myself from being hit. I had made it through abuse, homelessness, and devastation. I had faced my father and gotten myself out of the relationships that nearly killed me. I chose to change my life just like I said that I would all those years ago. I had lived so long feeling completely trapped. I finally built my own door and walked through it. Perfectly timed because I then met the love of my life.

When the right man walks into your life and loves you the way you deserve to be loved, your whole perspective on life will change.

— Amari Soul

7

I FOUND LOVE

*M*ark. We were just kids when we met. I was 18 and he was 19 and he became my true love story. I went to a continuation school for several months after I moved in with my mom this last time for a short period. While I was there, I met a guy who I had a little crush on named Jeff before I met his brother Mark. Jeff told his brother, "There's this new girl in school and she's really hot; you need to come and check her out." Mark and Jeff pulled up at the school one day in Mark's gold Volkswagen. They stopped me to say hi. I thought Mark was cute but I remember thinking that he was way out of my league. I still weighed 80 pounds and was just coming off the streets. I had very low confidence in myself and thought, *Why would this good-looking, buff guy have anything to do with me?* I wouldn't meet Mark again until he and my good friend Kathy would race their Volkswagens a short time later. We went out in the country on a back road in Oakdale so they could race. I got to be the flag girl. I was excited to stand between the cars and signal "GO!" As I whipped the flag down, the cars sped past me. Mark always recalls how much he loved my Daisy Dukes. I don't know if they were Daisy Dukes, but in Mark's fond memory, they were. Again, we only met briefly, and I was just getting everything straightened out in my life so I didn't pay much attention. I happened to catch a glimpse of him in the coming weeks while I was driving. I saw him pick up his girlfriend as she stood outside of a Taco Bell. I know it was small but it stuck with me. I saw his kindness even in that quick moment. Then on April 21, 1982, not long after the drag races, we connected. We have been connected ever since. I went to "the Cove" that sat at the back of the Oakdale reservoir. This is where kids would go to party and race their cars. My friend Kathy and I were at the cove to race her Volkswagen again when Mark pulled up in his friend Glenn's car. You would have thought a celebrity had arrived. About 20 girls were rushing toward him. The girls were yelling, "It's Mark Joiner! Its Mark Joiner!" I couldn't believe it. He was tan (well, he's Greek and Italian, so he's always tan) and his body was like nothing I had seen. He took care of himself, he worked out, and he was really buff. I remember thinking, *Oh my God, who is this guy? He is hot*. I obviously knew who he was, but everyone's reaction was wild. I didn't want anything to do with him because I knew he had all these girls who liked him.

He also had an ex-girlfriend and I had lived a lifetime by the time I was 18. I knew that getting involved with someone who had a high likelihood of a jealous ex wasn't a good idea. I was intrigued but I would not let him know it. I stayed back, not rushing the car. First, I had been through hell, so that was never going to be me. And second, I had my guard up. Despite the many girls hovering around him (he'd already been kissing one girl) he walked over to me. He tried to make small talk and then boldly asked if I'd want to take a quick ride with him to the store. My instinctual reaction was *no* and my thought, as I recall, was something along the lines of, *No, I'm not going to the store with you, jerk*. Don't ask me why, but somehow, he changed my mind. I felt nervous inside. I had been in the car with strangers since I was 12 years old, I had hitchhiked alone as a child, I had fought and survived men twice my age who had almost gotten the best of me. And Mark *made me nervous*. I wasn't afraid of him; I was afraid of what I was feeling. I said yes to the store because I wanted to know more about him. Was he really a nice person? Handsome, athletic, and kind? Honestly, that scared the shit out of me. It would turn out that Mark was all of that and so much more. We became inseparable. To be clear, I did not make a minute of this easy on him. I had more walls up than even I could climb but knew I really liked him. In fact, I told Mark within a few days of spending time together that we didn't need to be serious, but no ex-girlfriends. I refused to feel like I was competing or dealing with drama. He gave me butterflies in my stomach.

Everything about him was different than anyone I had known. He was a gentleman; he opened every door for me and does to this day. I knew I loved him much sooner than I could even admit to myself. My sister Rachel and I had gotten an apartment by this time and it was 30 minutes away from where Mark lived. I really began to believe he loved me when he rode his 10-speed bike for miles to come to see me when his car was taken away for not having insurance. He brought me flowers and jewelry but what mostly set him apart was that he always treated me with love and respect. I found myself picking up a few pieces of myself that I thought I had lost forever.

I was so afraid to meet Mark's family. He took me to meet his mom and dad in Oakdale only about 30 minutes away. Before I even met them, I kept thinking, *I don't want them to find out who I really am.* I felt broken inside. What would they think of me if they knew I was practically from the streets? I was so relieved when his mom was instantly so warm and welcoming. I still felt like I needed to hide my past. I kept my answers general and without a hint of trauma. Mark's mom says that when she met me, she thought I was very classy with my high heel shoes. She also says that I thought my shit didn't stink. Ha-ha! She really liked me. Mark and his family were saviors to me during that time, and I truly don't think they could ever understand the healing magnitude of their love and kindness toward me at that time in my life. When we first got together, Mark didn't believe most of my stories about what I had been through and the things that I had done. He had no idea that I came from the streets and that I lived a horrible life prior to meeting him. It wasn't that he thought I was lying; he just truly couldn't picture me living that way.

His family wasn't perfect, of course—every family has issues—but they were perfect for me. They modeled the kind of family unit I had wished I had in my life growing up. Mark grew up in San Francisco and most of his family still lived there. When we would go visit, I would think back to when I had come to the city for modeling jobs and dreamed of a new life filled with possibility. I felt that life that I had imagined starting to unfold when we would go see them. The whole family did things together—spent time with grandparents, had large and boisterous family get-togethers. They also reminded me of my life in Arizona, before it fell apart. My parents had 22 siblings between them and our family gatherings during the good times were large, with lots of laughter. They modeled for me a lot of behaviors for which I had no reference. Even small things, like the ability to apologize for wrongdoing or to have an argument that didn't end in walking out, stunned me. I couldn't remember my parents ever apologizing, and nobody sat down and worked through problems. As much as I loved Mark's family—and still do—I was also a little envious. I looked at his parents compared to mine. They had been really good to him. They really loved him. But even though I felt so shattered on the inside, Mark's family loved me too. His mom, especially, treated me like her own daughter. She showed me the love that my mom couldn't. I am forever grateful for this beautiful, big Greek and Italian family. They made a place for me at their table and I made a place for them in my heart.

Mark always went above and beyond for me, which stood out in sharp contrast to the guys who had come before him. But one of the greatest gifts he gave me was time spent with him and his family. I don't know if he knew it, but it meant more than I could express at the time to get to be around a family that was different, in all the best ways, from my own. We were married 10 months after we met and are happily married 37 years later. Mark and I would end up going through so much together, but we made it, and we love each other even more now.

Mark asked my stepdad and my mom for their blessing and they both gave it. Even they could see what a great guy he was. He proposed to me with a beautiful little ring with a flower and a diamond center. Mark's aunt was my maid of honor. My dad was forbidden from attending. We were supposed to get married in August after he proposed, but we were pregnant before then so we moved the timeline up. Tenisha, our firstborn, was conceived by two people madly in love—in a gold Volkswagen.

Although I loved Mark with everything I had, it took years for me to trust that he wasn't going to hurt me or leave. Even after we got married, I put up walls. When we would fight, I was always the violent one. He would never harm me, even though I repeatedly tried to goad him into it. I think I was trying to get him to leave me. I remember swearing at him, telling him to leave me or divorce me. And I'm so thankful that he didn't listen to me and he chose to stay even though on occasion I acted like I didn't want that at all.

It's funny how I think about that now, but back then, I had no concept of what I was doing. I was just living in my anger —waiting and watching for him to turn into just another one of the guys I had dated before, who cheated on me, hurt me inside, and beat me. But Mark never did. He's the love of my life. Even after 37 years of marriage, my husband cooks me dinner. He gets up every morning and makes sure my car is warm in the winter and cool in the summer. He walks me to the car and carries my bag. He brings me lunch. He truly takes care of me and I'm very grateful for him. His favorite saying about our marriage is, "Yes dear, a happy wife makes a happy life!" I truly believe and know in my heart that nobody could ever love me as Mark loves me. Even on my ugliest days he always tells me I'm beautiful! Our marriage would be put to the test over the years, but our love has always been too damn strong. It wins every time.

My story is filled with broken pieces, terrible choices, and ugly truths. It's also filled with a major comeback, peace in my soul, and a grace that saved my life.

— *Unknown*

8

A FIFTH-GRADE EDUCATION

I will say this, I learned a lot of valuable lessons throughout my tumultuous dating past, that all culminated into one simple fact: I must control my own life. I would never be trapped, homeless, hungry, or abused again. EVER. I decided early on that no man was going to have power over me, whether that power was to smack me around or break my heart. If I wanted something, I was going to go get it myself. I'm not going to wait for anyone to do it because they might not. So from the get-go, I controlled everything in our finances because that way I knew that, whatever happened, I would have a way out if our relationship didn't work. Mark never displayed any sign that I was not safe, but this wasn't about Mark. This was about me knowing that I had the power to never be victimized again. That's something I knew from experience that not every woman is able to do, and I didn't ever want to put myself in that position again.

When we first got married, we moved in with Mark's mom and dad. We were so grateful but it was extremely difficult. I was pregnant and I had been on my own for so long that it was difficult to live with people. I began looking for an apartment for Mark, the baby, and me to move into. We worked aggressively on getting enough money together to move out. I had a job at Thrifty's and Mark worked at New Deal Market. We moved out shortly after our daughter Tenisha was born.

Tenisha came two months early. It was traumatic. There were serious complications for both Tenisha and me. I had to have a C-section because my placenta had ripped and moved in front of my cervix. The baby wasn't going to come out. I had to have emergency surgery, and while in surgery my lungs collapsed from an onset of pneumonia. Tenisha had to stay in the ICU for over a month. I couldn't see her for the first five days of her life because of my pneumonia. Mark was right there by my side for everything. I realize we were just kids back then when I think of our friends who came to see us. I remember Mark's best friends Glenn and Rick laughing so hard because as they rode in the hospital elevator, they pretended to get into a real fight, arguing over which of them was "the real father," just to get a rise out of bystanders. They had fun, but I was having a really hard time.

The first moments after a baby is born are some of the

most important for bonding. I have always wondered if Tenisha and I being forced to separate for that time impacted us. I was a wreck for those first days of not being with her. I cried and cried. I felt a deep depression inside. I can say Tenisha has an iron will just like her mom. We butted heads over the years and she has grown into one of the most remarkable women I know, and my little grandsons are right on her heels. *A note to my daughter: you're one of the greatest gifts I've ever gotten.*

When we were finally able to bring Tenisha home, she cried a lot. She did not stop crying for months. But we finally had our own little home.

I loved our little apartment on 6th Street. I took pride in not only working but also being able to keep a good, clean household. I think partly I got that from my mother, that innate respect and desire for a clean and decent living space. Interestingly, when we were kids (before all hell broke loose), it was "yes, ma'am" and "no, sir." We sat still and quiet, knew how to respect adults, and understood the value of a clean home. Further, I had a home—my own home, to live in and care for. This satisfied a deep need in me to feel safe. I belonged somewhere without question. I loved having our apartment for more reasons than I can even name. I was married, a new mom, in love, had a decent job and had a place to call home. I was definitely making good on the promise I had made to myself to turn my life around at 18. I was nervous about being a mother and a wife. After my childhood and the relationship I had with my mom, I began to worry about what kind of mom I would be. Plus, I was still only 19 years old, and no matter how much life I had lived, I was still a kid myself. I knew a few things for sure: I would always protect my children, I would love them with all I've got, and I would do everything in my power to make sure they never went without or had to go through what I went through.

Tenisha had colic, and I don't know if Mark or I slept for a year. Her esophagus took time to form so I was covered in and reeked of baby projectile for a year, because everything she consumed came back up. She was only 17 inches long and weighed four pounds, six ounces when she came home, and her little bones were so fragile. The bones in her skull took time to develop so everything with Tenisha had to be handled with extreme care. We were on, around the clock. Mark was able to get a good job working for 7-Up and I was able to stay home for a couple of years, taking care of Tenisha, who had become hell on wheels, and our precious son Mark, whom we call Marky, right behind her.

Our apartment had been a great stepping-stone, but I really wanted a house. We moved into a cute little home on 2nd Street in Oakdale. We were on our way, but what I really, truly wanted was for us to own our home—not rent it. Owning a home meant security to me. I didn't think of it like this then but I believe my desire to continually increase the level of our security and safety was a constant undercurrent for me. I had a financial ambition that I wasn't shy about discussing and it was rooted in my desire to guarantee our family would never be on the streets. I wanted a house, and though Mark didn't see a need for the rush, I persisted. When I was 23, we bought our first house. We had about $3,000 in savings from Mark's parents. We were just $200 short. I had become great friends with our neighbor, Papa Ed, as I called him. He lent me $200 and I paid him back every penny. The resourcefulness I had cultivated as a child would continue to serve me well through life. We had enough for a down payment on a brand-new, 1,040-square-foot place in South Modesto. One of the companies I own today is a real estate company. I think back to the 13% interest rate on homes back then and just can't believe it. We moved into our beautiful home and it was a dream come true. I had been home with the kids for a few years now and money was tight to make ends meet. I would pick up shifts at JCPenney to help, but I knew we needed more and I wanted more—more security. I didn't want us struggling. I've always liked working. The feeling of being in charge of my destiny and doing what it takes to create it was in my blood. I had made it this far and I wasn't anywhere close to stopping. Mark had a stable upbringing with a loving family and homelessness was fortunately nowhere in his reality. Mark would have been happy where we were because we really had a great thing going, but because of where I had come from, I needed to put as much distance between me and crisis as I could. That was going to take more education, more hard work, and making a lot more money. I needed a career or at least a job that I could really help pay our bills with. I knew I had a fifth-grade education. I had gone to tenth grade for a very short stint just so I could receive my driver's license, but the truth was I didn't really know how to read or write. I know it's hard to imagine how I made it even that far without being able to read, but I was a strong communicator, and Lord knows I was innovative, so I had just always figured out what I had to. But getting a really good job without being able to read was a tall order. I was committed. I then received my first break and I took it. I applied to work as an optical technician at an optical store in the Vintage Faire Mall in Modesto. As I went through the interview my stomach was in knots. *Is he going to require me to have my high school diploma? Is he going to find out I can't read? If he gives me a chance, I know I can do this!* My mind was racing. The gentleman who ended up hiring me that day, Eric, may never understand the chance he gave me. He certainly didn't know I didn't have my diploma, but he opened a critical door in my life that day. This young girl, young wife, a young mom with a battlefield behind her and without knowing how to read was given the chance to really change her life. I showed up every day and I learned fast and I worked hard. I felt so proud in my white lab coat. I began grinding lenses in the lab and learned to use all of the equipment. It was official—I had landed my first really good job and I gave it everything I had. Working in a lab and working on a skill that I actually enjoyed learning began to unlock the doors of endless possibilities in my mind.

Becoming a working mom was tough on us. Mark and I had Tenisha and Marky who were basically toddlers at this time. We shuffled childcare and schedules, we lacked sleep—we were strained, to say the least. As hard as it was, to me, nothing had ever felt so good. I knew I was trying to lay a solid foundation and Mark did too. We made it work like we always have.

Through moving around in the optical field, I started to alter the way I viewed myself and my education. I was operating with the tiniest minimum of education, but I realized as I began working that my lack of education had nothing to do with my intelligence. My confidence in my ability to learn continued to increase at a rapid pace. For the first time, I began to understand that I was smart. I may not have been traditionally educated, sure, but I was an excellent student. In fact, looking back on all the scrapes I had gotten myself out of and all the practical skills I learned—albeit under terrible circumstances—I had become pretty damn smart.

I ended up working at a warehouse that manufactured and sold eyeglasses. I was promoted to quality control, which came with a pay raise. This was great but I wanted to go higher. I decided it was time for me to get my ABO license (optician's license with the American Board of Opticianry). This would prove to be my greatest early accomplishment. I couldn't read well enough to study for the exam, so I memorized the definitions by making up my own words and used word association to memorize what word defined what. I literally cut out and pasted words and meanings together and memorized them like pictures. I studied in every spare waking moment. I had heard stories around the warehouse about how some people had taken the test multiple times and had never passed, even after working in the field for years. The lady who sat next to me at work was also about to take the test. She had been there for far longer than I, and she was worried sick, and she could read! I didn't let any of this stop me. I just knew that if I worked hard enough, I could do it. That test was like my diploma for me—if I could pass it, it would be tangible, real proof that I could do something correctly and well. Deep down I felt that if I could do it, I could do anything.

Walking into that test room may have been the most afraid that I had ever been and, as you know, that is saying something. My hands were sweaty, my heart was racing, everything in me was shaking. I remember thinking, *Who am I to think I can pass this when I can't even read?* For me, there was so much more riding on this than a grade. This was evidence that would prove to me that I have what it takes to do this life on a completely different level.

When I learned I passed the test, I was elated. In truth, there aren't words to fully describe what that moment meant to me, but I took it and ran. I had been moving with momentum until that point, but when I passed the exam, I was no longer running toward my goals—I broke into an outright sprint. I was becoming unstoppable. In my heart, I knew that I was going to keep going so far and fast that the life I had come from would be crushed by my level of perseverance and success. I needed to never feel powerless again. I realized then I had never been stupid; I just hadn't had a chance to learn. Now that I had removed that limiting belief, I then asked, "What else is possible?" We were overseeing more than 750 jobs a day and now that I had my license, I had made an abrupt entry into a man's world with unequal pay. I was being paid nearly 45% less per hour than the men in the same position. This was not okay with me. I wanted to be able to control my own future and how much money I made. My father ran an entire business while drunk; there's no telling what I could do since I wasn't living that lifestyle. I was not my father in any way, but as I've said before, he was a hard worker and that I will give him. That success pushed me to set goals for myself, to push through my own self-doubt and establish my own life's purpose. I wanted to own my own business. I made the decision then that I would own my own business by 30 years old. The entrepreneur in me had awakened.

I choose to believe things are possible, even when I don't know how they will happen.

— Jack Canfield

9

LIMOUSINES...YES

$\mathcal{V}$ision. I've isolated possibly the single most powerful part of how I've achieved the milestones I have over the years. I see my goal in my mind—the final result in its entirety. The rest is me doing whatever it takes to build the road to get there. I may not know how or have the resources when I initially see the vision, but I have never let that stop me for a second. If I would have needed to have it all figured out and been certain that I wouldn't fail before I stepped toward each goal, I'd still be homeless. My childhood showed me that where there is a will there's a way. It's not a cliché to me. It has been a lifeline in a sea of uncertainty. I decided I was going to open my own business by the time I was 30 and I did it. I didn't know what kind of business but I knew I was going to do it. Originally, I considered opening a restaurant but as I got further in, I knew it wasn't the right timing for that. I kept searching for what I would really go after. First, and most ironic, was that my father won the lottery—a million dollars—and in case you're wondering, he did not give me a dime and I'm not sure I would have taken it if he had. He had actually become homeless himself after I turned 18. He lost his company and that awful house, but winning the lottery changed all of that for him. He planned to use some of his winnings to open a limousine company. He never made good on that idea, but it sounded great to me, so that's exactly what I decided would be my first business. I told Mark about my idea and he got on board. He was nervous about what seemed like a wild idea but he supported what I really wanted. I took money out of my 401k that I had built up working as an optical technician, and I bought a 1989 Lincoln Town Car limousine and started driving it at night and working at the warehouse during the day. This wasn't my first rodeo with a car company. Friends of ours, Brad and Tracy, also owned one, and I used to do runs for them when my schedule allowed it. In fact, that first Lincoln Town Car I purchased was one of the cars I drove for our friends. I was committed to making the company a success. To give you a glimpse of my level of commitment, I'll share a funny story that always reminds me of what it looks like to be all in. I had gotten a call to take several high-end clients to the airport. Many people need limousines from all walks of life and for many occasions, but these happened to be the kind that could probably just afford to have a limo service full time. The job was in the middle of the night, at 4:00 a.m. in the morning. I drove up to the house of the first client. Brad had told me, "When you go into her driveway, go in at an angle. She lives down below the cliff at the bottom, and there's no gate around her driveway, so be careful." I slid off the cliff slightly as I drove down her driveway and got stuck. The lady was down below asking me if everything was alright. I said, "Not really. I need to call Brad and he needs to bring me another car." In the meantime, I was still trying to get myself out of this mess by trying to dig with a piece of wood I found to dislodge the car, but it was hopeless. So Brad showed up with another car. The client and I proceeded to the next lady's house which was on Warnerville Road in Oakdale. We pulled up and I opened the glove box to pop the trunk. The lady got out of the passenger side and I got out of the driver side. I heard the client yelling, "Marie! Marie!" The car was rolling as I turned around. I grabbed the car door and in a split second, I was sucked down underneath the vehicle. As I was being dragged down Warnerville Road, I was thinking, *I'm going to die. How I am going to get out of this? If I let go of the door it's going to hit me in the head.* I just said to myself, *Let go and lay as flat as possible,* so I did, and the car rolled over my legs and my feet and the door scraped my side. Now I was flat on the road looking back as my car was still going backwards down the road. I felt like the wily coyote when the roadrunner ran him over, "Beep! Beep!" My adrenaline was rushing. I got up and ran after the car. God only knows how I stopped it, but I got inside and I put the car in park. Now I was crying over the steering wheel, and the first lady I had picked up screamed, "Move over! I've got to get to the airport!" and then she was taking over my vehicle. The guy in the house was yelling, "Is everybody alright out there?" and all three ladies were yelling back, "Everything is just fine!" I was thinking, *No, call the ambulance, I am not fine.* She pushed me to the other side of the car and drove us to the third home in Riverbank. We pulled up to the home and she parked the car. I said, "Look, I can't let you drive the vehicle. I will take it from here." I got out of the vehicle and proceeded to the front door and knocked. The lady answered, and I introduced myself: "Hi, I'm Marie and I'll be your chauffeur this morning." She got a scared look on her face, in disbelief. I was covered in dirt and had mascara running down my face. I'm sure there was also blood. I grabbed her bags and as I was walking away, she said, "Hey, your underwear is hanging out of your pants." It was from the car dragging me down the road. Well, we still had one more lady to pick up before we were on our way to the airport. Finally, I had everyone in the car and we were en route to the airport. I heard the lady from the first house say to the others, "If she was dead I would have shoveled her off to the side of the road, taken the car, and I would have called Brad and told him to pick his car up at the airport." One of the ladies closest to me saw I was bleeding from my shoulder and handling a Kleenex. I stayed professional and friendly and dropped them off at the airport. Then I wanted to pass out from the pain. Now that is commitment!

It still cracks me up that I ended up buying the car that ran me over. It's also interesting to note that on that same road, Warnerville Road, I had gotten in that car accident in the Nova with those scary men. My life was coming full circle in the best way. This time I drove down that road completely determined to succeed and I had come too far to let anything stop me. The limo company was only supposed to be something on the side, but it started to really take off. I had to decide — play it safe, or quit my day job and start driving limos full time. I chose to dedicate all my time to my entrepreneurial pursuits. It was getting to be too much to drive limos at night while also working a day job; I was exhausted driving all night and working all day. I had to sleep at a friend's house near where I was dropping off clients to barely get enough rest to make it to work on time. I don't even know sometimes how Mark and I did it during those years with the kids and our schedules, but we did. We were utterly exhausted, but by God, we did it. That wasn't the only factor working against me during the formation of this new company. I still wasn't able to functionally read or write, so Mark had to fill out forms and documents for me for years. After I got my first computer, I started learning how to read through the Microsoft Word program and a brutal amount of trial and error. Thank God for the spellchecker.

When I started focusing solely on the limo company, it

was like I was a woman possessed. I was so driven that I would take any call that came, regardless of day or time. It could be one, two, or three o'clock in the morning and I would go. Mark would be so irritated with me, leaving the house in the middle of the night, but I was determined to make this work, and intuitively I knew this was the level of commitment I had to have to see it all the way through. This level of commitment built the number one limousine service, Luxury Limousine Service, that has now been successfully growing in size every year for the past 25 years. When I first opened my limo company, everything presented a learning curve. I had to learn how to navigate the ins and outs of a successful customer service model, how to keep the books (in an era before computers, with no GPS and no cell phones). I still managed to grow my business from a $900 profit the first month to $75,000 in the first year. I think back to my jobs with Montgomery Ward and JCPenney and will always be grateful for the insight I received regarding customer service. Luxury Limousine Service has grown significantly every year. I sometimes wonder why I have pushed myself so relentlessly to constantly improve. I keep telling myself I'm going to stop starting new ventures, that I'm perfectly fine with mastering what I have going, and then I go and start another business. Partly, I think it's because I get bored; once I master something, I want to try something else. Partly—maybe more than partly—I have never let myself just relax in my success because the little girl in me that didn't have food, a home, or safety just won't risk complacency. Maybe part of me has never been certain the other shoe won't drop. And just in case, I'll never be caught off guard. It seems silly to some people that I'm always working with my head down, trying to figure out how to learn and work and hustle. It's ingrained in me at this point, I think. I want to learn and try to eventually master whatever it is I'm working on. A lot of people I've met have the attitude that they can't ever do what I do. Maybe they can't, but how would they know unless they try?

I never had any idea how to do anything I attempted, whether it was getting my ABO license, starting a limo company, or getting my broker's license. I credit my childhood for my ability to learn what I needed to learn and to do what I needed to do. Whenever I needed or wanted something, I had to learn how to get it for myself. For better or worse, I learned early on that no one was going to do anything for me, and I had to force myself to not give up in order to get what I needed or wanted. I know from experience that everyone is going to fail. Failure is nothing more than a tool for your own success. If you fail, don't give up—just take it as a lesson and keep moving forward.

Pride is a block to learning, in my opinion. If you want to learn, you have to be willing to ask a lot of questions. Most of my learning was done by picking brains, sitting next to the smartest person in the room and asking them questions. Reading a book wasn't something I could do, although I did listen to some books on tape to keep myself awake when I was driving nights. I never took classes to learn about business. I did not have a high school diploma. Hell, I didn't even graduate from the eighth grade. So I was never allowed to take any college classes.

Everything I've learned in life was *self-taught*. I started expanding my business portfolio. I wanted to do mortgages. For this, I would need to also have my real estate license. There would be more stepping-stones to cross and tests I would have to pass. I drove about two hours one way to learn from a little blonde spitfire who taught me everything I needed to know. Again, I asked hundreds of questions—maybe even thousands. Eventually, I was able to successfully do mortgage loans and get my real estate license. It took so many hours of studying for me to achieve these milestones. My reading and writing had improved but it still challenged me to my core. See, the vision I had was to also own my own real estate company, Bella Casa Realty. I had come up with the name nearly six years before it would come to fruition. Today, both Luxury Limousines and Bella Casa Realty are thriving. So naturally, I'm currently opening a wine bar and event center and becoming an author because I can't help myself! But I'm also shifting into a new gear. More enjoyment, more family time, more peace. It took me some time to get here.

I love you unconditionally and forever. No matter what."
   — Marie

10

SO MANY HATS

*B*eing a wife, mom, and business owner is a lot to juggle for anyone. There is no rule book or perfect way, and it's usually in hindsight where areas for improvement become clearer. My children Tenisha and Marky are grown adults now with lives and dreams of their own. We all made it through and are actually entering into a really great place where I get to be there for them and their little families. As they grew up, I worked hard to provide for my children the life I wished I had as a kid and the life I felt they deserved. No matter how hard I tried, I could not be in more than one place at one time. I desperately wanted to be at every event, party, and special occasion, but I missed a lot of those. In retrospect, my focus was more primal—keeping them safe, fed, clothed, and ensuring they never felt less-than. I wanted them to feel well taken care of. I didn't ever want them to know what it felt like to have old, beat-up clothes, be embarrassed at school, or have to hustle for a seat at anyone's table. I love them with all of my heart and I tried to show them by making sure all of their needs were met. I made sure they had rules and I would fight for those rules and structure, because I knew what could happen if no one was waiting up for them. I didn't want them to have to depend on anyone who could take advantage of their needs. I didn't get to spend the kind of quality time I wanted with them, however. All throughout their growing-up years, I hustled and hustled, starting and maintaining one venture after another, in order to purchase them the best clothes and cars and vacations. But they didn't want those things; they wanted their mother. Whether they could understand it at the time or not, they had all of me. Every call I answered in the middle of the night, every move I made, every test I studied for—it was for them. I was going to protect them no matter what. It's not right or wrong; it was the best I knew. When my son was old enough to start partying, he did. I panicked and tried to block him at every turn. I know they both felt like I was intense. I *was* intense—I had steered us out of a life they would never have to know and I would keep it that way at all costs. I was definitely the "bad cop" between Mark and me. I was always so afraid. My fear didn't ever look shaky and timid, though; in fact, if I was scared, I looked more like a lion. I worried about whether how hard I worked had made the kids feel emotionally abandoned sometimes. I just didn't know how to do it all. And if I had to choose between their safety or their game, I chose their safety. No matter what I did I felt guilty. Sometimes I wonder if that's just a side effect of being a mom. Damned if you do, damned if you don't. Loving my mom was like loving a porcupine and I had to, very intentionally, let my guard down enough to let my kids in. Everything took learning for me. They were and are amazing kids, though. I really was struggling inside with a lot from my past and it really showed up when Tenisha was 12 years old. I started reflecting on my life and my childhood compared to my daughter's childhood. And I realized how innocent she really was and that's the way I should've been at age 12. It rocked me. I saw what had been happening to me by that age under a different light. For the first time, it gave me permission to feel devastated over it all. I had just launched myself out of that old life and didn't dare let myself stop and look back too long. But somehow seeing her young and happy, the pain from my childhood was in my face. I decided to seek therapy. I was starting to figure out the toll my childhood and past was taking on me and was realizing that I wasn't going to change unless I got my shit together with someone else. My father's renewed presence in my life only underscored that need.

When my kids were young, my dad moved in with us. I only allowed him in my home because he was homeless and had nowhere else to go (this was before he won the lottery). His alcoholism had gotten so out of control that he wasn't able to hold onto a job. I remember marveling at how he had hit an even lower rock bottom. The man who lost a leg and still founded his own business, who maintained a steady flow of drugs and alcohol and outperformed all his workers, had finally actually hit rock bottom. Even though it was my decision to take him in, it wasn't easy for me to live with my decision. That's an understatement. I was spiraling internally, to the point of shaking, with him there. I would sit on the end of my bed feeling physically ill because of my proximity to him. I was angry all the time, ready to lash out at him at the slightest inkling that he may be doing something wrong. He was dating a prostitute who would show up at my house, strung out on heroin. Her johns (paying customers) would call my house asking for her. These were the same kinds of people that I spent time around when I was a kid. This was all entirely too close to home for me—literally and figuratively. So I kicked him out, back on the streets. I wasn't going to let his lifestyle into my house and around my kids. No way.

I knew enough about myself at that point to know that I was a mental, physical, and emotional mess. I had gotten past the point of "stone-faced," so I was feeling things, but I was feeling so much that it pushed me quickly toward a breaking point. I thought about suicide a lot. Not seriously—I wasn't planning to kill myself or anything—but in a passive way. Like, if I didn't wake up the next day, that would be fine because at least I wouldn't be in pain.

I even wrote my daughter a letter. Mark actually found it recently, in my jewelry box. I wrote it when I knew that I wasn't okay, but I didn't know how to fix myself. I had convinced myself there was no way I could be a good mother when I was so troubled and traumatized. Objectively, I was a good mother. I had my issues, as every parent does, but I gave my kids a better life than my parents gave me.

I saw a psychiatrist a handful of times and got some good stress-management skills out of the deal, that I did take to heart. The therapist kept telling me that I needed to confront my father, who at that point was living in Nebraska after having won his $1 million lottery and had bought a five-bedroom home for $500,000.

My younger sister Renee and I flew to Nebraska. Once we got to Nebraska and to my dad's home, of course, he was drunk. We went to the park to talk to him. I laid it all out on the table. I told him that he was a terrible father and that he knew that all of the things that had happened to me with his friends were wrong. I told him how angry I was that he had done nothing to ever stop it or help me. I said my piece, not thinking he heard me because he was so drunk. I didn't even think he would remember me being there. I went back home with a little sense of relief that he knew that I knew. About six months later he called me to apologize. He shared that he really knew what he had done and that he had been a terrible dad. From that day forward I was able to forgive him. I was able to move forward without hating him. I had always carried such guilt—I had feared that if he died, I would hate him. I couldn't love him as I should, but I forgave him.

That was the day I realized how freeing forgiveness is. The more I could forgive people for how they'd wronged me, the more I was able to feel more whole.

I tried to have a similar conversation with my mother a little more recently. We were sitting in the living room of the house I live in now, and I told her that I was angry with her for doing the things she did when I was a kid. I explained to her that the reason why I had moved in with my dad in the first place was because she incessantly spoke poorly about him and I was angry with her for that. I was stuck in the middle of their fight. I wanted to be given the choice to decide who my father was going to be to me, and I saw her as removing that choice. Further, she had turned our life to shambles and Jim was so violent.

Unlike my father, my mother was not contrite or remorseful. She got very upset with me and said she hated that I was even bringing any of that up. I wish I could say otherwise, but I really wasn't expecting anything else from her in terms of a reaction. My mom was always closed off, so frankly, I was surprised I even saw that kind of a response from her.

In many ways, I learned how *not* to be a parent from my parents. There were many things I could point to about both my mother and father that I knew I didn't want to carry to my own kids. I gave my children structure in the way my father never did. I tried my best to better myself so I wouldn't turn out like my mother. She never sought therapy, and I think she would have been able to be a better mom if she had. So I went to a psychiatrist and did everything I could to take care of myself and continue to take care of my kids with the healthiest version of me. Then something happened so far outside of my control that in one night the family I worked so hard to protect was almost lost.

Strong women aren't simply born. They are made by the storms they walk through.

11

THEY STOLE MORE THAN OUR JEWELRY

*I*n 2003, I was running my limo company, the mortgage company, and Mark and I had just opened a restaurant. Things were always a little hectic with schedules, multiple businesses, and life, but everything had hit new solid ground. Things were good until one August night. We were robbed in a home invasion.

The robbery began at about 3:00 in the morning. We were all asleep with the exception of my son, Marky, who had come home late and was sitting in the living room, eating a hotdog and talking to his friend on the phone. We didn't lock anything up back then. We lived in the country and right by a busy road, so we felt perfectly safe leaving our windows open, especially in the heat of summer.

Unbeknownst to us, there were three men outside our

house watching my son talking on the phone. When Marky got off the phone, he heard them coming through the door. Mark and I were awakened from a dead sleep by two masked men with flashlights in our faces, swearing at us to "get out of the fucking bed." One of them hit Mark in the head with the barrel of a gun. Mark got out of the bed first and they threw a towel over his head. I remember putting my arm over my head thinking, *Oh my God, this isn't real.* The nightmare only became real when Mark started telling me, "Get out of the bed, MARIE!" They threw a towel over my head too. I reached for my sweats at the end of the bed but couldn't see with the towel covering my vision. I was only wearing my bra and panties. I could see there was blood on the floor. As we walked, I was struck with terror that someone had been shot. I remember screaming for my daughter. I felt like I was going to pee my panties as they walked us into the living room at gunpoint. My daughter's room was right next to our room. I looked in there and could see a guy getting her out of bed. He had a mask on his face—a white-and-black bandanna. They led me into the living room. I was in shock and disbelief that this was happening and so scared at the same time.

I could see my son as they were grabbing him off the couch. As he was going down, they were hitting him in the head with the barrel of the gun. He was saying, "Hey dude! Hey dude!" And after that, I heard nothing. My daughter was screaming at them, "Leave me alone! Leave me alone! I'm pregnant!" I can remember just telling everybody, "Shut the fuck up and do what they tell you to do." My daughter was so brave.

My worst nightmare was unfolding. Safety, protection, violation, victimization, powerlessness. Everything I had fought against and made it away from against all odds. Everything I had worked to the bone to save my family from. These three men with their cowards' masks and their guns had gone for not just my jugular but my entire family. I was terrified, but I became laser focused on one thing, and my entire childhood had prepared me for it—survival. We had to survive.

They laid us face down on the living room floor next to my son and tied us up. They started ripping our rings off our fingers. They left my daughter untied because she was pregnant and left Marky and me facedown while they took Mark back to the bedroom. They wanted to know where the safe was, but Mark didn't know. I did, because I had just moved the safe out of our closet and to another room of the house.

When they realized this, they left Mark in the bedroom and came back for me. As they untied me, they told me that my story of the safe's location better match my husband's story or else they would kill us both. I led them to the safe in our weight room. As I opened the safe, I scooted away from it. There wasn't any money in there—just jewelry which wasn't taken because they didn't see it. I didn't have any cash in the house. They grabbed me and took me back to the living room. They tied me back up. From my vantage point, I could see them kicking my husband in the back of the head over and over. There was so much blood. Then they came to me and put a gun between my legs and put the barrel of the gun up inside of my vagina while telling Mark that if he didn't tell them where the money was, they would "blow the bitch up." I was freezing up; all I could think was that I was about to die. But I had to stay calm. I was so scared and almost blurted out that I was getting $100,000 in a couple of days from a real estate deal. I remember telling myself, *They don't know!*

Eventually, they figured out that I was the one in the house who knew where the money was. They untied me and took me into my office. But because I didn't keep cash in the house—I put it all in the bank as soon as I got it—I could only offer them what we had on hand, less than $40. I reverted back to my old self and reminded myself that if I kept in check and didn't say anything, I could survive anything I went through, including this. If all of the monsters in my closet had taught me anything, it was that I could make it out. I just had to stay calm, do what they said, and make it out alive.

They started cutting my undergarments off me. I remember dropping to the floor of my office, wondering what was going to happen to me as one of the robbers asked me if I had ever cheated on my husband. I knew they were beginning to play mind games with me, so I told them I had a driver coming to pick up a car in a few minutes—which was true but not for a few more hours—and hoped that would be enough to get them out of the house. I told them I had $37 and they took me back into the living room. I was virtually naked. I don't think they believed me. They were still beating Mark, then they took the barrel of the gun and put it next to his head and started playing Russian Roulette. They pulled the trigger, again and again, and every click would nearly stop my heart. They put me in front of the loveseat, facedown with my butt sticking up in the air, with one of the guys pretending to rape me. You could feel the evilness of the devil himself in our home. My son, I later learned, was watching everything that was happening to me.

They told Mark they were taking me with them. I heard a deep sigh come from Mark. One of them put me over his shoulder and they took me out to the back patio. By this point, I had no clothes on. They tried repeatedly to drown me in the hot tub, trying to get me to give up where our money was. The whole time, I was trying to figure out, *What do they want from me? I've told them we have no money in the house. What do I say to get myself out of this?* They kept telling me I was prejudiced, trying to make me believe they were black to cover their true identity. I told them I was not prejudiced, that I once was engaged to a black man. Once I said that one of them said, "Ew." I knew at that point he wasn't black. He was playing more mind games with me. I knew from my past life that I needed to make them see me as a real person. If I became humanized, they would find it harder to continue the assault.

They brought Mark outside next and tried to drown him too. As they continued to hold our heads under water, I could see all of the blood throughout the hot tub. The water was becoming a darker and darker red. I, for sure, thought we were going to die. I repeatedly insisted that we didn't have any money in the house, that it was all in the bank.

Mark tried to fight back. He had broken loose from his restraints. I screamed for him to stop after they stuck a gun to his head and told him they were going to shoot him. There was so much blood everywhere, I thought that we actually might not live through this. Eventually, they took Mark and me back inside where they first threw me on the couch, and they tied Mark back up. Then I was forced to my daughter's room where they put me on the bed, one of them standing behind me repeating, "Bitch, quit crying, bitch," and covering my face with a pillow. The other man standing in front of me was holding a knife to my stomach, forcing my legs open, and raping me with the end of an object. I was in such pain as I cried. The louder I cried, the harder he pushed on the pillow covering my face. It was getting harder to breathe. I remember lying there crying, and thinking I actually was going to die this time. I knew immediately when they had pulled me from the couch earlier what was going to happen to me. *Here we go. Here we go*, I said over and over again in my mind. I survived Jimbo and so many others. I would survive this. When they were finished, they brought me back out into the living room and put me back on the couch. And then the robber's phone rang. *Thank God.*

They had a driver outside waiting for them and they had been inside the house way too long. I didn't want to look at them because I was afraid that they'd kill me if I saw their faces (even though they were covered by masks). But I remember seeing them, all in black, standing over me. At this point, they had been in our house for probably an hour, violating me, beating my husband, and with my son and daughter being traumatized.

This is where God comes in. I started praying, asking Him to get us out of this safely. As they laid me down in the living room again and tied me up, I could feel something like a shield come over us. They had put a blanket over the top of us. One of the men tying me up said if we moved, there was someone at the door who would shoot us. Three of us didn't move, but my daughter did. She got up and walked to the back door the second the guys left. There was no one there.

My daughter untied us. I ran to the weight room to get the one phone with the only wires the robbers hadn't cut and called the police. I was wrapped in a blanket and I remember my son saying to me, "Mom, you have no clothes on." I went into our bedroom where they had turned everything upside down and found a t-shirt and put it on. I went into the bathroom and sat on the toilet. There was blood everywhere. Once I came out of the bathroom, I remember sliding down the wall to the floor, crying and saying, "I think it's Anthony." Later, I found out that one of their names was Anthony.

The police later said they had never seen anything so horrific, especially in the case of a home invasion like this. Ours was the latest in a string of robberies but was decidedly the most violent they had ever seen.

Ambulances arrived to take us to the hospital but I was adamant about not going. I had a driver coming to pick up a car and I still felt a responsibility to my business and my clients. I know I was in shock. The police convinced me that I needed to go. I just kept telling them to take my family and that I'd be alright. Despite all the horrors my family and I had just gone through, I knew even then it would not destroy us. My driver arrived at the house to the sight of ambulances taking his boss and her family away.

Even now, almost two decades later, people still try to talk to me about that night. I tend to brush them off or say it's really not the time and place to be discussing it. Though we've all made full physical recoveries from that night, the terror and loss of safety never fully goes away. We all felt violated. It's a pretty traumatic thing for someone to come into your home — the place where you're meant to feel safe and protected — and hurt you and your loved ones. We lived in fear for a long time after that. I would sit outside my house in my car with the doors locked when I came home late at night, afraid to go inside until Mark came home. Still to this day I am aware of my surroundings. The fear has never fully left. We never sleep with our window open. We had an alarm system and cameras installed in the house, which helped me feel a little safer, but my whole family dissolved into dysfunction after that for a period of time.

We all had our own serious issues over what happened to us. We gave up the restaurant after the robbery. We were all drinking a lot more, trying to block out what had happened. My husband, who initially had no idea that I had been sexually assaulted, and Marky, who had witnessed his parents being beaten and assaulted, had a really hard time. Tenisha had put on a remarkably brave face, but none of us came through that unscathed. Mark and Marky weren't backing down from anything because of what happened. They would fight each other. They would fight anyone who looked at them wrong. They had felt helpless that they could not help their family or themselves. Their drinking had escalated, and this was how they were coping with what happened.

I was also traumatized, but I sought help and went to see a psychiatrist again and had both Tenisha and Marky go with me. I tried to get Mark to go but Mark was going to deal with his own issues in his own way. Whenever someone talks about the robbery it brings up a lot for him. My daughter handled it calmly in the moment and during the immediate aftermath. But of course, it haunts her too sometimes. It brought on PTSD for her and certain things will trigger it.

All three of the robbers and their accomplices were eventually caught after a shootout with cops in Turlock, after their last home invasion. They were put on trial for a string of robberies, home invasions, assaults, and rape. They were with the Nortenos gang. I remember sitting there in court and looking at them, realizing just how young two of the men were —20 and 21 years old. They had lived their young lives like mine, and I felt sorry for them, knowing that they never had a chance. Their parents were part of the gang and the home invasions.

I got a little bit of satisfaction out of the trial. One of the robbers wanted to stand up and plead his innocence, and when he did, I convinced almost every victim and everyone in the courtroom to stand up and walk out. My vindication came in that no one would be there to witness this criminal's statements. It felt pretty good, honestly, like it was a start to my healing. They called me Jane Doe throughout the trial. When the trial was over and a reporter was asking me questions, my first reaction was, "My name is Marie Joiner. I want you to print it. I am a person and not a Jane Doe. This happened to me."

FORGIVENESS is not always easy. At times, it feels more painful than the wound we suffered, to forgive the one that inflicted it. And yet, there is no peace without forgiveness. – Unknown

I had to forgive them, just like I did my dad. I had to let all of it go because all it was doing was making me fall apart even more, and I had to keep it together for my family. Even now, years later, I still cringe when people bring it up to me. It's usually at some sort of function that people look over at me—

even to this day, many years later—and ask me or Mark about it. It's never easy to hear those questions; I'm never sure how to answer them. You can usually see it on my and my husband's faces—our demeanor changes instantly. It brings up a traumatic part of our lives. A part that we try not to think about anymore. I've even had a few people try to tell me in their own opinion what happened to us, in our home. I have had others tell me that they'd have "shot the robbers" with their guns. They would have never let them leave alive. I would think to myself, *Sure, when you are in a dead sleep and rendered helpless and they have guns. My family did exactly what we needed to do to survive. No one knows how they are going to react in that kind of situation.* During the robbers' next home invasion, they used our guns that they had stolen from our home and shot the victim five times because he fought back, and he almost died.

Moving forward was a process—a long one. I gained a new perspective and a sense of immediacy. Little things didn't matter as much as they once did. I started appreciating all my challenges and reframing them under the umbrella of "I survived a home invasion, so this is literally nothing." Once again, I had to make the active decision to forgive the people who caused me so much hurt, because carrying it around was just going to harm me. I had to learn how to be kind to others, mindful of my impact on others, and strong for my family, even while I was seething with pain and anger.

Throughout my life, I've had to be strong. Strong enough to survive my childhood, strong enough to pull myself up after realizing the kind of person I didn't want to be, and strong enough to overcome the traumatic events of my adulthood. My choice to be strong made me a different person—someone more positive, someone who chose to actively pursue better things, who wanted to try her best to make something more of herself and her life.

I cannot let anybody take me back to a place I prayed my way out of.

12

THE LAST PIECE FELL

I chose not to let the robbery define me and my life. I had already triumphed over my childhood, and I decided that just because someone had attempted to ruin my life, I was not going to let it drag me back to that dark place. I had fought too hard for too long. The robbery happened, sure, and it was horrible and terrifying, but I didn't die. So it was my responsibility to keep moving forward and to do my best for my family.

Marky was completely traumatized by the robbery. He started drinking, which threw up all kinds of red flags for me. I was seeing a pattern repeat itself. My son, who looked like my father, was going down the same path he did. Our robbery was in August, and in November of the same year, Marky was with his cousins Justin and Jeffery. They were all drinking. Marky decided to get behind the wheel of his sister's little red convertible BMW and ended up getting into an accident on the freeway. His cousin was thrown out of the vehicle and into the oleanders on Highway 99. Fortunately, they were not injured. This would be Marky's first drunk-driving experience, but it would not be his last. The hits kept coming. By January, Marky was diagnosed with testicular cancer. After removing a testicle, they discovered the tumor was benign. The summer after the robbery, Marky, while drunk, climbed up onto a roof. He was at his girlfriend Marissa's house. Her parents were out of town and the kids were over there partying. Marky, being drunk and the daredevil he was, climbed to the peak of the roof of the house. It was about 35 feet off the ground. He went to jump into the pool, but he slipped on the tile roof and landed head-first on the cement, then into the hot tub. His friends got him out of the hot tub and called an ambulance. Then his girlfriend Marissa called Mark and me to let us know there was an accident. "Marky is hurt badly and he barely has a pulse." We of course rushed over to her house. When we arrived, they had Marky in the ambulance and would not let me go with him. This led to the culmination of all my pain and anger. It was too much. This event set off a cascade of emotions and events that nearly destroyed my family.

When we arrived at the hospital, the doctor took us to a back room and shared that he wasn't sure our son was going to be okay—that he was most likely going to be paralyzed for the rest of his life. I sat quietly as the doctor spoke. I reverted back to the "stone-faced" Marie who had endured so much on the streets, in my father's home, and with the recent robbery. I stood up while the doctor was still talking and went into the bathroom. Everything in me just broke. You could hear me scream throughout the entire hospital.

I remember beating on the bathroom floor and screaming and hitting my husband when he came in to get me. I told him to let him die. Marky wasn't going to be okay being paralyzed; he would want to die. The pain inside me was so deep that it went to my core. It made me physically ill. When people came to the hospital to see Marky, I would avoid them; I would hide in a corner and pray for my son. I had spoken to God throughout my life but never like this. It had been less than a year since we had been robbed. The robbery became nothing in the face of my son lying in the hospital, near death. Marky had broken his neck, blew out his fifth and sixth vertebrae, split his head open, broken his eye socket and damaged his spinal cord. He would have to have surgery to replace the two bones with donor bone and put a titanium plate in his neck, along with fusing the fourth, fifth, sixth, and seventh vertebrae together. He would be put in a halo to keep his neck still for months. Marky only weighed 70 pounds before it was all over with.

He was put into an induced coma until he had his surgery. Once they started bringing him out of it, he couldn't recall anything that had happened. Every time Marky would wake up, he had amnesia. He had a tube down his throat, so he couldn't speak. We had to tell him what happened to him again and again. He would mouth the words "stupid, stupid, stupid" then fall back to sleep. We had to keep reliving it for him because he didn't remember. I think that might have been a blessing; it gave him some peace, although it cracked this mother's chest open every time I had to tell my son how he might never walk again. This was it. *This would officially mark the hardest thing I would ever face, that Marky would face, that our family would face.* I just wanted to die. It wasn't an option and, ironically, I would need to be stronger than I had ever been. No amount of work or success could fix this. I just needed to keep it together for my son as he went through the darkest hours of his life. I would pray over his body starting from his head down, asking God to fix his spinal cord, to make him whole again. I envisioned God's hands touching his spinal cord and healing it. Then I would start praying on the left side of his body, hover my hand over him and work my way to the right side. By the time I got to the other side, I would be praying less. I tease him now, telling him that's why the right side still has a little paralysis, and *it is your reminder from GOD not to take life for granted*. We've had to have some dark humor in our house to get through.

Marky's recovery was slow but miraculous. He started being able to move his toes, and little by little he regained mobility throughout most of his body. He had to learn how to do everything all over again. He went through intense therapy to learn how to walk again. I can't even imagine the amount of pain and frustration he was in during that time, not having any autonomy, having to be fed, bathed, and dressed.

After we brought Marky home, things escalated emotionally. Mark was drinking pretty heavily between the robbery, Marky's cancer scare, and now this. He had hit the limit. Marky, understandably, was enraged by what had happened to his body and life. In one year our family went through hell. Marky's anger was directed toward me verbally as I was the one closest to him. Between the frustration of his inability to take care of himself and the influence of his medication, it just got so bad. So I left. Not for long—only about a week—but for the first time, I gave myself permission to step back and put my own oxygen mask on. I told Mark that I wasn't mentally or physically able to take care of our son, and that he needed to take care of him because my mental state was declining rapidly. For so long, I had been the strong person no matter what—the mom who tried so hard to make everything okay. But I wasn't okay, and I needed to fix myself before I could help anyone else.

Mark and I even split up for a few months. He temporarily moved out of our home. We had a second home from an earlier investment and he stayed there. He was drinking and imploding to cope with his grief and trauma, and I wasn't willing to endure anymore. I learned the hard way that we all have highs and lows in our lives, and the way we handle them, more than anything, defines what we are going to get out of life and what we are going to make of ourselves. Sometimes we can hit some low lows—and we were there—but there is always a chance to come back stronger than ever, as long as you still have a pulse.

Mark and I were separated for about six months before we got back together. The robbery and Marky's accident nearly ruined us. I believe if you love someone in the beginning, you can love them in the end. Mark and I experienced a kind of hell together that we both had to find our way out of. We both felt like we couldn't protect our family, our children, or each other from something so terrible happening. The robbery left us feeling raw, angry, and vulnerable. But Marky's accident— we couldn't bear what had happened to our son. We fell apart and then we fell back together. That gorgeous guy who stepped out of his friend's car that day at the cove was and is my soulmate. The flag girl with her Daisy Dukes wasn't giving up on him or us. We have never given up on anything and we absolutely weren't going to start with each other. Mark and I made it through some of the deepest waters a couple can wade through, and today we get to enjoy the fruits of our labor. When you fall in love with someone, you have to try to rediscover those things you love about them whenever adversity strikes. We worked on moving forward together, then and for many years after. He was there for me, encouraging me through thick and thin. Through economic crashes, company pivots, and all the ups and downs that come with business, Mark was there to love me when it all felt like it was too much. He's been there for me when I've needed him most—as kids, as young adults, and at every pit stop along the way.

Marky kept drinking for about 10 more years after that terrible night on the roof. As I watched his decline, I kept urging him to stop drinking and to keep away from other substances. I spoke from personal experience, because I knew what his future looked like if he kept going down this road, and I didn't want to go through what I went through with my dad. I would constantly pray for him and send him all kinds of inspirational and get-your-shit-together type quotes. Showing him tough love, I tried everything in hopes of sinking it into his head that he could make it out stronger than ever. As a mother, it was killing me to watch my son losing his life to alcoholism. I loved him and couldn't lose him.

Today, I am so grateful and proud to tell you that Marky turned it all around and has become a remarkable man. He fought his way out of his darkest hours and came out on top. *A note to my son: A dog is a man's best friend.*

If you are struggling today, remember this: You have survived everything you've gone through up to this point. The best days of your life are yet to come. There are still people you haven't met, and things you haven't experienced. YOU CAN DO THIS!

— Unknown

13

WHOLE

*F*or so long, I felt like my life had shattered and even when I repaired it on the outside, I still felt like I was broken on the inside. I was scared that the pieces of myself had been scattered too far and wide to ever find them all. I didn't give up hope and I have picked up all the pieces one by one. For the first time, I feel whole. I still try to instill in my children and everyone else I interact with that a lack of knowledge is no excuse, and a clear vision backed by a strong work ethic can make you unstoppable. There are many times in my life that I haven't known for a fact how something was going to happen, but I worked at making it come around anyway. Remember, I had the name "Bella Casa Realty" in my head for six years before I started that business. Instead of using my childhood and background as an excuse to fail and stay stagnant, I held myself accountable for what I wanted and I used other tools to get to that point.

There are a lot of affirmations that I use to stay motivated. For example, the old man I met when I was 12 who told me that being a grownup is great because *you're responsible for your own destiny.* These remind me that I am capable and strong. Words like these from an unknown author help keep me accountable:

She has been broken. She has been knocked down. She has been defeated. She has felt the pain most couldn't handle. She looks fear in the face, year after year, day after day, but yet, she never runs. She never hides. And she always finds a way to get back up. She is unbreakable. She's a warrior. She's you.

I've thought for a long time about how I can help other people through my story. We don't have to have the exact same trials to relate to the feelings of hopelessness or the desires found in our dreams. I've made sure that I have the means and ability to leave situations that don't serve me, which was not an option I had as a child. I have a friend, Tracy, who is a teacher at the continuation high school in Ceres. She has asked me if I could come in and talk to a girl who's pregnant and whose boyfriend is beating her. She has also asked me to speak to her class on several occasions. While I understand intimately what the pregnant girl is going through, I also know what she must be thinking. For her, there may be no immediate way out. But at least my story can empower me to empower her with the hope that if we are willing to push forward, no matter what, we can make it up and out of anything. Everything is a moment in time and "this too shall pass," but you have to fight your way out of it. Be strong knowing that life does get better.

Even when my life was at its worst, the one thing that saved me was that I had to become more. When you start to realize and acknowledge that every struggle is a stepping-stone to a lesson in life, then life stops feeling like it's against you. You have to look inside that lesson and find the answer to your next movement forward. We all have struggles in life and it's what you do with each one of those that counts. I'm one of the few in my family who have gotten their lives together. I have achieved the most in my family on both sides, setting a completely new level of possibility for the generations after me. Even still, I live with guilt surrounding my family members' situations. Just the other day, one of my nephews reached out to me and asked me to send him money because he was about to end up in jail. It wasn't the first time he asked for money. I told him, just like the old man said to me when I was 12 years old, once you become 18 you control your life, not your parents. I've been telling him and his older brother this since they were young boys, hoping that this would stick in their heads and they would get their lives together. We all have choices! The choices that you make become the outcome of your life. So choose wisely! I reminded my nephew he has three young children and it was time for him to get his life together. Because if not, his children will grow up just like he has grown up, and those children will have children fighting the same battles. He needs to be the one to break the chain. It's never too late to start, so start today.

As I chose for myself and my family to have a better life, they had those same options once they were 18 years old.

I'm a giver. I have empathy for other people's lives. I can see and feel others' pain that most people cannot. I do have boundaries I have set for myself. I will give you a chance to move forward, but if you're moving backward, I will let go.

It's hard to know when to hold a firm boundary in hope that the person will learn they have wings, and when to step in and help. I'm still working on the guilt that comes along with this, and I'm learning to allow myself to live with the consequences of my family members' actions. Sometimes it almost feels like survivor's guilt.

Out of my entire life story, I hope people can understand that living with nothing is better than living in a mess. You're in charge of your own life and your own story. You and only you can choose how to move forward. I did everything that I did because I made choices that led me, baby step by baby step, into the life I've chosen. I'm not saying it's easy, because it's not. But I think people tend to make excuses for themselves. You have to be tough and you have to be willing to step forward even if you slide back. You can sit around feeling sorry for yourself and say woe is me, or you can pick up those pieces and succeed. If I can pick up the pieces, you can too.

Breathe in and let go of your past so you can live with courage in the future!

  - Marie Joiner

Not The End--XO